PEOPLE BEHIND THE PEACE

People behind the Peace

Community and Reconciliation
in Northern Ireland

RONALD A. WELLS

William B. Eerdmans Publishing Company
Grand Rapids, Michigan / Cambridge, U.K.

Published 1999 by Wm. B. Eerdmans Publishing Co.
255 Jefferson Ave. S.E., Grand Rapids, Michigan 49503 /
P.O. Box 163, Cambridge CB3 9PU U.K.

Printed in the United States of America

04 03 02 01 00 99   7 6 5 4 3 2 1

Library of Congress Cataloging-in-Publication Data

Wells, Ronald, 1941-
    People behind the peace: community and reconciliation in Northern Ireland /
    Ronald A. Wells.
        p.   cm.
    ISBN 0-8028-4667-X (pa.: alk. paper)
    1. Northern Ireland — History. 2. Peace movements — Northern Ireland —
History — 20th century. 3. Reconciliation — Religious aspects —
Christianity. 4. Community — Religious aspects — Christianity.
5. Peace — Religious aspects — Christianity.
I. Title.
DA990.U46W45   1999
941.6 — dc21   99-18022
                                                              CIP

For Barbara
Channel of Peace

Contents

Acknowledgments

I t is standard form for an author to thank those who gave assistance in the making of a book. In this instance it goes beyond graceful convention to mention certain people. The main subjects of the book — the Christian peace-seekers of Northern Ireland — are the first ones to be thanked. These people, busy doing good work, gave generously of their time and ideas. Also, during my many visits to Ulster, I came to depend on the goodwill and encouragement of friends, especially David and Frances Livingstone, Tom and Grace Fraser, Duncan Morrow, and Trevor and Carys Morrow.

Calvin College, in the form of both a sabbatical leave and a grant from the Alumni Association, made the book possible, for which I am very grateful. Thanks are also due for the encouragement from the friends at my publisher, William B. Eerdmans, especially Jon Pott and Charles Van Hof. I thank Donna Romanowski and Lynn Vander Wall, who were cheerful and helpful in manuscript preparation. Finally, my wife Barbara, to whom this work is dedicated, and who believed both in the project and in me during a difficult period of illness, is thankfully acknowledged as the person who has shown me grace and peace.

R.W.

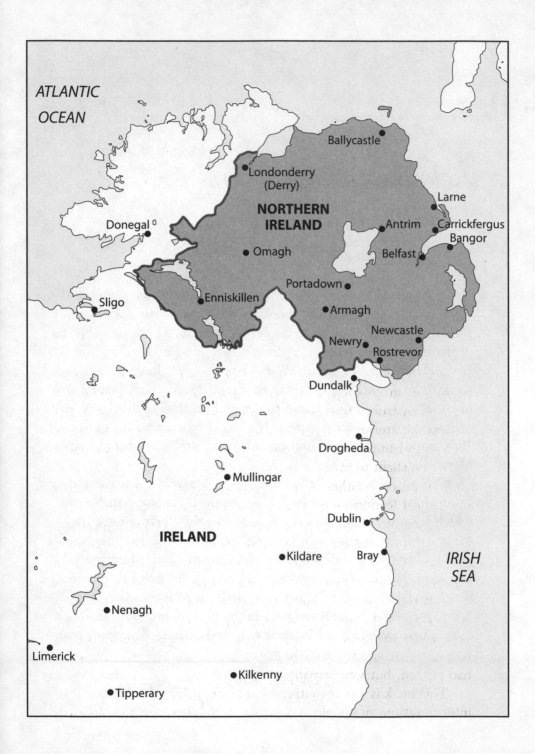

Religion as Cause and Cure of Conflict in Northern Ireland

Orientation Points

In this book I hope to tell the stories of some Christians who were important in creating the context in which the politicians were able to construct a framework for peace in Northern Ireland. In selecting the stories of the people at the Corrymeela Community, the Columbanus Community, and the Christian Renewal Centre, I intend no slight to other religious folk who contributed to the creation of peace. Neither would I undervalue the courage and vision of political leaders — especially John Hume, David Trimble, and Gerry Adams — who were so important in the breakthrough that occurred on Good Friday, 1998. But, one must focus somewhere, between large generalities and a plethora of specifics that would leave readers overwhelmed by details. When I focus my camera, as it were, on Northern Ireland and the peace process, this is what I see. This is a story that I believe is worth telling because it gives witness to the work of those who, by their costly faithfulness, helped to make the breakthrough toward peace for which many had prayed, but which many also had feared would never come.

This book is also a continuing corrective for the repeated misinterpretations of people and events in Northern Ireland. Journalistic and academic commentators have, for several generations, refused to see what was right before their eyes — that is, that the conflict in Northern Ireland has been about religion. Now, having said that, one quickly qualifies the comment by pointing out that the conflict is not solely or merely about religion. To engage in a fully orbed evaluation of the Ulster conflict, one must discuss politics, economics, social class, and gender. But it has been typical of most journalistic and academic analyses to suggest that religion did not — indeed, could not — figure prominently in "the troubles." A large part of the tendency to see religion as only a symbolic issue, and not the real issue, turns on the failure of imagination among many, if not most, journalists and academics to understand and appreciate the continuing impact of religion in the modern world. In some other places I have discussed at length and with care the various ways in which religion was a vital factor in "the troubles," so there is no need to do that here.[1] But, for current purposes, a few points need to be made.

Religious worldviews and the actions that spring therefrom are important in understanding the conflicted behavior of the people of Northern Ireland. While this is perhaps somewhat more true for Protestants than Catholics, religion is a major cause of social dysfunction for all concerned. While religion energized ideologies about society, the nation, and "the other," it also became captive to them. In the conflict that has broken out with renewed ferocity since 1969, religion has provided a way to mark the boundaries of the mind and spirit as much as political boundaries have. But religious worldviews and values have also been at work in Ulster among those who have tried to break down boundaries between people. The religious folk who are the focus of this book fully appreciate the difficulties and dilemmas that religious peacemakers have encountered in places like South Africa, El Salvador, and

1. "A Fearful People: Religion and the Ulster Conflict," *Eire-Ireland* 28 (Spring 1993): 53-68; "Protestant Ideology and the Irish Conflict: Comparing Ulster Protestants and American Evangelicals," *Fides et Historia* 23 (Fall 1993): 3-17; *Ulster-American Religion: The History of a Cultural Connection* (with David Livingstone) (Notre Dame, Ind.: University of Notre Dame Press, 1999).

Croatia: that religion was both cause of and cure for social conflict. Indeed, precisely because religion was so important in causing the conflict, religion was also to be vital in finding the way to peace.

I noted above that religion has been and is important for setting boundaries for the mind and spirit as well as for the land itself. It is true that every person, institution, and society needs some boundaries to maintain a sense of identity and worth. We all need to come from somewhere, be related to specific others, and believe in something if we are to function well. But the definition of who "we" are is the matter at issue. One reading of the Christian story from the Bible involves appropriating God's favor for our own tribe, people, and tongue, and ascribing negative qualities of being "outside" God's favor to "other" tribes, peoples, and tongues. But — and this is vital — according to an alternate reading of the Bible, the essence of the Christian story is that God's favor is meant for all people. Thus viewed, the task for faithful ones is to proclaim the message of liberation from the confinement of particularity and contingency to the worldwide community of those who name the Name.

What is at stake here is progressive revelation. Early in the biblical story, God seems to bestow his favor exclusively on a particular people. As the story unfolds, however, and especially after the resurrection of Jesus, the good news is predicated on God's favor to all. Finally, in the last biblical testimony in the book of Revelation, the universality of God's grace is revealed. Those who name the Name, who will sing the praises of the Almighty in endless songs, come from all tribes, peoples, and tongues. There will be, of course, the final boundary marking the faithful from the faithless — heaven and hell are still Christian doctrines — but the inhabitants of the two will not be chosen according to the human contingencies of politics, nationality, race, class, and gender.

All Christians share a common prayer, the Lord's Prayer. (The Reformation did not change that.) About the plea to God ("thy kingdom come") that all Christians utter, we do well to consult the Bible about what that kingdom will look like. Scripture says that the kingdom will come in the morning, when time shall be no more, when all the tears will be wiped from our eyes, when the lion and the lamb will lie down together — when, in short, there will be "shalom." God, it seems, does not prefer a certain race (whites will not be over blacks) or gender (men will not be over women) or nationality (Serbs will not be over Croats) or social class (the powerful will not be over the lowly and meek) or denomination (Presbyterians will not be over Catholics).

The two readings of the Christian story are both plausible. One can see that in the Old Testament God's favor was exclusive, while in the post-resurrection era God's favor is inclusive — some would say universal. It is, I think, not so much that God himself changed his mind, but that the record we have of his revelation seems to develop over time. By the end of the Bible, God desires that all peoples come to him, to live in his favor and at peace with each other. This interpretation will cause its contemporary adherents to see their task very differently from those who view their task as trying to maintain the boundaries between those chosen and those beyond the pale.

The Plan of This Book

I began thinking about this book in 1990. My original idea was to tell the stories of the three residential communities engaged in peace and reconciliation. Please recall that in 1990 the Berlin Wall was still standing, apartheid in South Africa was still in place, and the prospects for peace and reconciliation in Northern Ireland were bleak indeed. I had hoped that my writing would be a witness to a peace that might come someday. I visited and resided in the three communities for varying lengths of time in the years since then. I was unable to complete this book in the early 1990s for several reasons, including personal illness, the press of other writing commitments, and a new administrative assignment at Calvin College. I had long wanted to return to this project. By the time I was able to do so, the Berlin Wall had fallen, apartheid had been dismantled, and — to the surprise and delight of nearly everyone

4

— cease-fires declared by the combatants in Northern Ireland had launched a peace process that was to bring the breakthrough on Good Friday, 1998. On that historic day, April 10, 1998, The Agreement (a comprehensive document that launched the peace process) was signed by all but one of the political parties.

Thus the ground had shifted significantly since this project began. Back then, no one gave a great deal of credence to reconciliatory activities. No one was talking about forgiveness in politics. No one could have foreseen the British, Irish, and American governments working so closely with the major parties in Northern Ireland, or have foreseen either the peace accord or the beginning of the elected assembly. But, looking back from this vantage point in late 1998, we can now see the movement toward peace really gaining momentum in 1995.

In 1995 the Irish Republican Army (IRA) proclaimed a cease-fire that was soon matched by the terrorists on the Loyalist side, mainly the Ulster Volunteer Force (UVF). This peaceful interval caused hopes to rise all around. But the British government either could not or would not encourage or push Unionist/Loyalist politicians into meaningful negotiations with their Republican/Nationalist counterparts. The cease-fire was broken in early 1996 by the IRA with spectacular bombings in London and Manchester, as well as much murder and mayhem begun again by several parties back in Ulster. Politically, the lost ground was not recovered until President Bill Clinton's personal emissary, former senator George Mitchell, was able to link up with the newly elected British prime minister Tony Blair (and his able colleague, Dr. Mo Mowlan) and the bipartisan leadership of John Bruton and Bertie Ahern in the Republic of Ireland. Only then could the hard negotiations that would point to Good Friday begin again in earnest.

Nineteen-ninety-five was also important because a significant book appeared from the noted American educator and ethicist Donald W. Shriver. This book, *An Ethic for Enemies: Forgiveness in Politics*, began a new and serious discussion of the usefulness of forgiveness in public life. I will discuss the impact of this book in the United States and elsewhere later. For now it is enough to say that the subject of forgiveness and reconciliation in societies of conflict like Northern Ireland is now a matter of open discussion in a way that was unthinkable a decade ago.

Also, from about 1995 onward, the patient peace-seekers in Northern Ireland began to believe that their efforts were yielding results. Not that they had not seen some successes before, but the pace of peace-seeking seemed to quicken as ordinary people, not just leaders, came forward from unexpected quarters to express new or renewed desires for peace. The ordinary folk of Northern Ireland, either because of new insights or because of their sheer weariness with conflict, began anew to seek the cross-community understanding that the peace-seeking communities had long promoted.

There was, in sum, a convergence of several things, from about the mid-1990s onward, that engaged the attention of this historian. As I mentioned, I had been interested for some time in the faithful witness of the peace communities. By the mid-1990s the whole matter of forgiveness was getting significant exposure. The political breakthrough of recent times had, therefore, legitimated what I had hoped for and believed: that Christian witness could have lasting societal and political impact. This book illustrates the power of that witness.

Readers who have "surfed the web" may treat what follows in (somewhat) like manner. Those who want to get right to the powerful and moving community narratives may want to read them first, and then come back to the other chapters. Those who want to be situated in the discussion about social and political forgiveness may want to read that chapter before getting into the community narratives. And those readers who feel a little disoriented about the political and religious history of Ireland and Northern Ireland may want to read the "history of the troubles" chapter before — or arguably after — the other chapters. In short, there is no "right" way to read this book. To use today's dreadful phrase, this book is "user-friendly." The chapters are related in such a way that a cohesive picture will develop no matter what reading order one chooses; seemingly diverse perspectives will converge.

Finally, the word "perspective" just used requires me to say a word or two about my own perspective. Most of the current books on Northern Ireland champion one or the other "side" of the conflict. This is a book about peace-seeking. I hope I have written it in a peaceful manner, and that people of diverse viewpoints can say — even if they don't agree with me — that I have represented the case fairly. I am a Protestant (though with a sprinkling of Catholics in my family's past and present). The book comes from a Protestant publisher (though one whose books transcend denominational differences). If this book succeeds at all, it will be because readers see as real the grace and peace of God that the subjects of the book seek.

A History of "the Troubles"

The question in Northern Ireland, asked repeatedly and urgently for at least a hundred years (arguably much longer), is a simple and straightforward one: What nation is this? It is an understandable enough question for people living in a modern northwest European country: Of what nation are we citizens? The fact that this could not be straightforwardly answered tells volumes about the troubled history of that land.

The national, or constitutional, question is the one under which all other Anglo-Irish questions are subsumed. The euphemism given by the Irish people to the societal turmoil resulting from the constitutional impasse is "the troubles." One could imagine a more dramatic term to describe social strife sometimes verging on civil war, but "the troubles" is the term used, so I shall use it too. I do so out of respect for the long-suffering people of Northern Ireland, who have the right to use their own terms, and also because the term honors the people's (perhaps unacknowledged) hope that their manifest social dysfunction is not, or will not be, as bad and as long-lived as some feared it might be. The term is probably just about right to describe a situation in which social strife and something like normal life co-exist. This paradox of day-to-day life continuing amid severe social dysfunction is something that non-Irish people find difficult to understand but that Irish people accept as a fact of life.

In view of all this, it is fair to ask, Can a nonpartisan history of the antecedents of "the troubles" be told? Absolute nonpartisanship is probably impossible, but fairness is not. In what follows, I try to give as fair a rendition of the historical context as is possible in a brief review.

Beginnings

Some observers insist that the beginnings of "the troubles" are traceable to 1916. Others would claim that 1690 is a more appropriate date. In fact, the arrival in Ireland of England's Henry II in 1172 first wove together two of the four strands that constitute the background of today's troubles. Henry brought his considerable army to Ireland as a precautionary measure because some of his barons had already settled in parts of that country and had become local rulers. Henry, fearful lest any of them should become too powerful and so threaten the throne, used his mighty visual aid to remind English and Irish alike that he was still the supreme power in the land. Since that time, England has been involved in Ireland as a civilizing or an oppressing force, depending on one's point of view.

Henry's excursion also introduced the religious connection. The Celtic Church at that time, while formally recognizing the authority of Rome, was both weak and independent. Reform, if it was to take place, needed the backing of a strong secular government. The pope therefore gave Henry's visit his official blessing in the hope that the king would set up a permanent, albeit foreign, administration. Thus, religion and its relationship to the state became a sensitive issue early in Irish history.

Having exerted rather than established his authority in Ireland, Henry turned his attention to other matters. Consequently, his influence and that of his successors began to wane until, by the middle of the fourteenth century, only about one-third of the country, mainly centered in Dublin, was ruled by the English crown. That is to say, most of Ulster, Munster, and Connaught had reverted to

Irish control. The English finally determined to stop the erosion of their power, but their policy lacked both the imagination and the drive necessary to tame the Irish. Put simply, the English problem was this: Wherever Irish and English intermingled, the Gaelic influence eventually predominated, and the English were absorbed. Their "solution" to the problem was the age-old one of separation, which was formally proclaimed in 1366. In that year a parliament was held in Kilkenny under the direction of the Duke of Clarence, son of King Edward III. The statutes it enacted touched most aspects of the people's lives. They make fascinating reading, for through them one can visualize the difficulties the two communities had in living together. The statutes included measures to improve the defenses of English-held territory, to prohibit private warfare, and to regulate trade. At the level of interpersonal relations, however, the restrictions imposed are even more revealing. Intermarriage between the communities and the fostering of each other's children were forbidden. The statutes also forbade the English, and those Irishmen who wanted to live with and as the English, to use the Irish language and Irish names, laws, or dress. They even banned the Irish practice of bareback horse-riding. Finally, they re-enacted existing laws that excluded the Irish from cathedral administration and religious houses.

The picture that emerges is one of a beleaguered and insecure English community among an alien people intent not so much on driving them out as swallowing them up, identity and all. In the light of this, it is worth noting how routinely these statutes were ignored. In fact, the church apparently exerted a greater influence on the people to obey the laws than did the state. The bishops threatened to excommunicate any who broke the laws, whereas the state had to import civil servants from England to administer them, so widely were they flouted even by those whose job it was to enforce them. England tried valiantly to strengthen its role in Ireland, but the separatist statutes of Kilkenny proved inadequate to safeguard English interests. One hundred years later, on Henry VII's accession, "the Pale" — the area of English dominance in Ireland — had shrunk considerably.

The Tudor Period

The accession of the Tudors to the English throne made little immediate difference in Ireland. Effective power remained in the hands of the earls of Kildare during the latter part of the fifteenth and early sixteenth centuries. This power was not democratic in nature but stemmed from ownership of large tracts of land and from political astuteness. The latter had caused the earls to enter into alliances with many neighboring Irish chieftains in an attempt to establish a durable peace. As a result, they were a natural choice to be the king's deputies in Ireland and to govern the country for him.

Periodically, and for various reasons, the earls forfeited the royal favor and were removed from their governing position. During one of these interludes, an important political event took place. In 1494, Sir Edward Poynings, the temporary deputy, called a parliament in Drogheda. From it issued a law that was to govern Irish politics for the next three hundred years. Poynings' Law, as it was called, prohibited the meeting of an Irish parliament without the prior consent of the king and council in England. Such consent, they made clear, would not be given unless they were first told why a parliament was being called and what bills were to be presented. This law made the Irish legislature essentially subservient to the English, and it was bitterly resented by many people. Thus, in a new and lasting way, politics, along with foreign intervention and religion, became the third strand that bound the two communities together in discord.

The English reconquest of Ireland started to gather momentum during the reign of Henry VIII. His coronation as King of Ireland in 1541 put Anglo-Irish relations on a totally new footing. It formally committed the king to Ireland in a way that had not bound his predecessors. At the very least, he was now obliged to defend and protect his fellow countrymen in that land. How much wealth he could recoup from Ireland also became a matter of royal concern. In Ireland the coronation radically affected the heads of family clans, whose ancestors had always been supreme in their

12

own land. It forced them to seek an accommodation between Henry's authority and their natural desire to remain in local control.

Henry chose the policy of "surrender and regrant" as the instrument by which he tried to implement his authority. Under it, the Irish chieftains surrendered their land to Henry, thereby acknowledging his leadership. He immediately regranted it to them to administer on his behalf, thereby protecting the chiefs' positions in their own communities. In an effort to guard against any undue independence by the Irish, a few restrictions were written into the regrants. First, the chieftains were not allowed to maintain private armies without the king's permission. This greatly reduced their potential ability to make trouble for Henry. Second, they were forced to follow and obey English customs and laws. By these means Henry attempted to persuade them to "think English" and to accept England's claim to rule them.

Henry's policy was, in the long run, as ineffective in subduing and integrating Ireland as were the statutes of Kilkenny, and for much the same reason. They were both English policies that took no account of Irish tradition. Henry's problem was that the heart of his policy, the idea of primogeniture — the understanding that when a leader dies, he is succeeded by his son — was foreign to the Irish. He had hoped, by including it, to ensure that the act of surrender would be honored through each succeeding generation. Irish chieftains, however, were traditionally men who had enforced their supremacy over all other claimants. Their rights to the land they ruled were certainly not hereditary. When they tried to make them hereditary, it was not long before the rank-and-file Irish rose up in opposition. The latter saw in the alliance between king and chieftains a move to deprive them of their land. In their view, any policy that cost them land, their only source of wealth, was a bad policy, and one to be resisted.

On the religious front, Henry's policy of "Catholicism without a pope" caused little stir in Ireland. The Irish chiefs felt no particular obligation to a pope, and the Anglo-Irish were prepared to follow the lead of their English brethren. Thus, both were content to support Henry's desire to be royally supreme over the church. In fact, the effect of Henry's edicts at the grass-roots level of Irish religious life was minimal. The Irish Church was weak because of internal dissension and poor because its ecclesiastical dues were often difficult to collect. Many of its churches were in ruins or in poor repair, and the religious teaching and ministering to the people's needs were undertaken mainly by itinerant friars. These clerics remained unaffected by Henry, since he produced no one to take their place. Even "his" English Bible — and, later, Edward's English prayer book — were in a language the Celtic people did not understand. So religious life continued largely unaffected by the major theological issues of the day.

When Elizabeth I came to the throne, she forced the Irish to accept her Protestantism by having it adopted by a parliament that met in Dublin in January 1560. The political consequences of this establishment of a Reformed church were soon apparent. First, the papacy, which had been England's ally in Ireland for the four hundred years since Henry II, became her enemy. Second, the new church attracted few supporters, and as a result Elizabeth's authority was decreased. To most of the natives and the Anglo-Irish, its organization and form of worship were foreign, and they preferred to continue to practice their own religion under the guidance of Jesuit priests who had come over from the continent. These priests developed strong personal ties with their parishioners and exercised great influence at the local level. (This ability to identify with and influence people locally still characterizes priests today.) The net result of the Reformation in Ireland, therefore, was more political than religious and very enduring. For the first time it caused the native and Anglo-Irish populations to work together to such an extent that, outside the Pale, national sentiment became associated with Catholicism. Today, four hundred years later, the association is still strong.

Elizabeth launched the third attempt by English monarchs to come to grips with governing Ireland. After the failures of the two Henrys, Elizabeth tried the policy of plantation. This involved taking land out of Irish ownership and giving it to English and Scottish settlers — those loyal to the crown — who were "planted" in it. The policy was first enforced in 1567, when, after the queen's armies had quelled a rebellion by local chiefs in Munster, large tracts of their land were confiscated and assigned to Englishmen. Elizabeth expected to apply her policy even more rigorously in Ulster after Hugh O'Neill, Ulster's premier chieftain, rebelled because of his increasing distaste for English laws, the Reformed Church, and the erosion of Gaelic traditions. Following O'Neill's victory over Sir Henry Bagenal at the battle of the Yellow Ford, Elizabeth sent the Earl of Essex to Ireland with twenty thousand men to reassert her authority. This he did in a long war of attrition, which ended six days after Elizabeth's death in 1603. Thus, the accession of James I to the English throne marked not only the end of the Tudors but also the end of the reconquest of Ireland.

1603-1800

Although Hugh O'Neill was defeated in 1603, the plantation of Ulster did not start until 1607. It was made possible by what has since become known as "the flight of the earls." The earls of Tyrone and Tyrconnell, two of Ulster's most important earls, decided that their postwar position had become impossible. While they had been allowed to retain their vast estates, they nevertheless felt that their power and independence were gone. In September 1607 they embarked for Europe, perhaps to seek military aid, taking many of their allies with them. Immediately their flight was interpreted as evidence of treason, and their estates, covering the counties of Armagh, Fermanagh, Londonderry, Tyrone, Cavan, and Donegal, were seized by the crown. Into these counties were shipped both English and lowland Scots settlers. The latter brought with them their own brand of Protestantism-Presbyterianism. The counties of Antrim and Down, on Ulster's east coast, were not included in the plantation; they had already been settled by people from the "mainland." Finally, in 1609-10, the city of Derry was "planted" by City of London companies, who changed its name to Londonderry. As a result,

City companies enjoyed extensive privileges in that area, including effective influence within the Church of Ireland. It is not hard to understand why the native Irish resented having their lands, and thus their wealth, confiscated and given to English intruders with a foreign culture and religion. Perhaps it was at this point in history that the whole question of wealth, and subsequently economics, became the fourth strand in the web of issues that together form the basis of the present difficulties.

Sir Thomas Wentworth, who was the king's deputy in Ireland from 1632 to 1640, increased the alienation between the counties still further. He harried the Ulster Protestants because of their sympathy for British Puritans, and he provoked the Catholic natives by continually seeking ways to deprive them of their land. However, his main contribution to the growing discord between the Irish and the English was in the field of trade. He actively discouraged the Irish wool industry, one of the country's few thriving industries, for no apparent reason other than to protect its English counterpart. This in turn increased Irish economic dependence on England, a dependence that was to have far-reaching consequences.

From 1640 to 1650, two significant events took place in Ireland, the first of which left a continuing legacy of bitterness. Oliver Cromwell, as Lord Lieutenant of Ireland, landed with twelve thousand men in Dublin in August 1649, with orders to reconquer the country after the uprising of 1641. Although he remained for only nine months, the cruelty and brutality of his methods, especially his sacking and razing of Drogheda and Wexford after the garrisons in those towns had refused to accept his terms, have not been forgotten. These events still form part of the anti-British bias within Irish Catholic folk history. The reason is threefold. First, it was primarily they who suffered under Cromwell; Protestants had rallied to his cause. Second, Irish Catholics further abhorred him because the "liberties" for which he fought excluded the liberty of saying mass — an act that could be punished by death. Finally, he saw himself as the instrument of God's wrath and judgment against them, even while he was putting two thousand of "those barbarous wretches" to the sword in Drogheda.

The second significant event of the 1640s was the establishment of a permanent Scottish Presbyterian ecclesiastical system in Ireland. For the first time, the Protestant faith was formally divided. Thus, by 1660, Ireland had three main religious groups: Anglicans, Catholics, and Protestant Dissenters, each with a different sense of history and each viewing the other two groups with suspicion and distrust.

The economic realities of life were made abundantly clear to the Irish during the latter part of the seventeenth century. The English parliament passed self-protective laws that excluded Irish cattle from the English market, restricted Irish trade with the American colonies, and further restricted their wool industry. Because the deprivation of market outlets was so serious, some people claimed that these acts, plus the flow of money to absentee English landlords from their poor Irish tenants, constituted a deliberate attempt to keep Ireland poor and subservient. Whatever the English motivation was, Irish resentment continued to grow.

James II fled to France in December 1688. Four months later, William and Mary were pronounced king and queen. These two events formed the prelude to one of the most famous milestones in Irish history. On his accession, James had made the brother of the Catholic Archbishop of Dublin the Earl of Tyrconnell, and had sent him to Ireland as his representative. By this act early in his reign, James had made clear his attitude toward the Irish. He needed their support for political reasons and devised his policy accordingly, despite the desire of a majority of Englishmen to maintain a Protestant ascendancy in Ireland. Within a short time Protestants were removed from the army, and Catholics were appointed judges and given control of restyled municipal corporations. Thousands of Protestants, apprehensive about the new policy, flocked to England to help dethrone James. Thus, it was not surprising that James, when he had collected an army with which to attempt to regain the throne he had lost during the English revolution, should start his campaign in Ireland. It was equally natural that the country's Protestants should unite to oppose him. Since most of the Protestants were in the north, the main opposition was centered in Ulster, most famously behind the walls of Londonderry and Enniskillen.

English troops arrived in August 1689 to raise the siege of Londonderry, and they, along with the Protestants, held off James's troops until William landed the following June. On July 1, 1690, William and James, the latter's army supplemented by an additional seven thousand troops from France, met and fought on the banks of the River Boyne near Drogheda (a battle now celebrated on July 12 each year, due to a calendar change). James's army was beaten, and subsequently it was decisively defeated at Limerick in October 1691. Because of the strength of religious feeling at the time, and because the politics of both William and James were intimately bound up with religious principles, William's victory was quickly credited with having rendered Catholics inferior in Ireland. The Protestant ascendancy was vindicated and assured for many years, and mythology and history combined to form the basis of today's religious intolerance.

This Protestant domination, bolstered by much overtly discriminatory legislation, was not undermined until the nineteenth century. Acts were passed that effectively excluded Catholics from the Irish Parliament and curtailed their right to acquire or lease land. Their inferior position was further underscored by the requirement that they pay tithes to the Church of Ireland. Nor were they the only unhappy citizens, for religious tests imposed during Anne's reign debarred Dissenters along with Catholics from public service. Thus the ascendancy, Anglican in character and socially divisive by nature, flourished in discontent and in increasing poverty that was made worse by further trade restrictions around the turn of the century. The very success of these discriminatory laws caused another significant change in Ireland. The numbers and influence of the Catholic gentry were so reduced that their role as political leaders and spokesmen was assumed by the clergy. Ironically, the laws thus tended to establish the powerful influence of the church they were designed to stop.

Jonathan Swift, in his magisterial work, *A Short View of the*

State of Ireland (1727), gave a graphic description of conditions in Ireland:

> It is manifest that whatever stranger took such a journey [through Ireland] would be apt to think himself travelling in Lapland or Iceland, rather than in a country so favored by nature as ours, both in fruitfulness of soil and temperature of climate. The miserable dress, and diet, and dwelling of the people; the general desolation in most parts of the kingdom; the old seats of nobility and gentry all in ruins and no new ones in their stead; the families of farmers who pay great rents living in filth and nastiness upon buttermilk and potatoes, without a shoe or stocking to their feet, or a house so convenient as an English hogsty to receive them — these may, indeed, be comfortable sights to an English spectator who comes for a short time to learn the language, and returns back to his own country, whither he finds all our wealth transmitted.

England, by right of conquest, exercised authority in Ireland. Yet by its extortionist policies, its harsh laws against the native Catholics and their religion, and its promotion of a Protestant ruling class, whose major qualification was its compliance with English views, England forfeited any right to be considered equitable, progressive, or humane. The bitterness engendered by the Reformation, the plantations, Cromwell, and the Battle of the Boyne grew during this period of relative calm in Irish affairs to form an indestructible and enduring core of resentment. This resentment was rooted in ethnic, political, religious, and economic bigotry attributable in large part to those who never considered themselves Irish.

It was not until the last decade of the century that trouble started to brew again in Ireland. In 1791, the United Irishmen organization was established in Belfast and Dublin by Wolfe Tone. This group, comprised of Catholics and Presbyterians, supported the twin causes of religious equality and radical political reform. They enjoyed some initial success when restrictions on Catholic education and voting rights were removed in 1793. Eventually, however, the United Irishmen became increasingly extreme in their demands, and in 1798 they joined the French in open rebellion against England. It has been said that their decision to make this alliance with France was prompted by the hope that, if victorious, Ireland would be granted her independence, as the French propagandists had promised. Yet it was this very alliance that doomed the rebellion to failure. For Ulster Presbyterians, no matter how strongly they disliked the English government, could not finally bring themselves to side with the French in an effort to create an independent Catholic, Celtic Ireland. Ulstermen, therefore, sided with the British, mainly through the agency of the newly founded, militantly anti-Catholic Orange lodges. The rebellion, which was ruthlessly put down, had severe political consequences. The Irish parliament was abolished, and an appropriate number of members of parliament were integrated into the British parliament Westminster by the Act of Union (1800).

The union was reluctantly accepted in Ireland. Protestants could see no other way to maintain their dominant position in light of the events that had so strikingly shown their dependence on English aid. Catholics accepted these closer ties with the old enemy, at least in part, because English Prime Minister Pitt promised them a Catholic emancipation bill as part of the union package. To Pitt, union seemed the only way to restore order and justice in Ireland. In the former he succeeded; in the latter he failed. His attempt to have Catholic emancipation added to the Union Act was defeated, for it gained little support in England at the time. Another twenty-eight years were to pass before Catholics were allowed to enter parliament, and the disenchantment and political agitation that occurred during this period contributed to the eventual failure of the union.

1800-1920

As the population of Ireland climbed to about eight million by 1840, their standard of living, dependent on the land, fell. Along with this increasing poverty there was an upsurge in sectarian violence. Members of the Orange Order became more intolerant, especially after passage of the Catholic Emancipation Act of 1829, and Protestant-Catholic animosity was encouraged on both sides by clerical and lay fanatics. One of the first modern religious riots, a forerunner of today's troubles, took place in Belfast in 1835. Two people were killed and others injured when soldiers clashed with people celebrating the anniversary of the Battle of the Boyne in Sandy Row, then, as now, a Protestant stronghold. At about the same time, Catholics were wrecking the Protestant area of Smithfield. Serious sectarian riots are also reported to have occurred in 1843, 1849, 1857, 1864, 1872, 1880, 1884, 1886, and 1898.

Andrew Boyd, in his book *Holy War in Belfast*, provides detailed descriptions of eyewitness accounts of the 1857 riots, which like many others took place during the "marching" season (the summer, when Protestants march in celebration of historic victories). The following descriptive statements have been taken from his account to show how discouragingly little progress toward community accommodation has been made in the intervening years. All these statements have appeared repeatedly, and in substantially the same form, in our newspapers over the past thirty years:

— There were emblems and flags (and) sectarian music.
— The mob from Sandy Row were taunting the Catholics and screaming insults about the Pope. The Catholics were equally abusive.
— The aspect of those localities was that of the camp of two armies, waiting only for a convenient time of actual battle.
— Gunmen had barricaded themselves in a nearby house.
— The firing continued every day from these positions, yet the police were unable to capture the gunmen responsible.
— The terrorizing of innocent individuals continued.
— [They] packed their belongings on a handcart and left Stanley Street never to return.

21

— The council of war decided that . . . the youngest and fittest constables would lay aside their heavy equipment and thus be able to pursue the mobs and make arrests.
— [They took] ammunition in the form of paving stones which they prised from the streets.
— The soldiers were hampered by army regulations.
— A special "Inquiry into the Conduct of the Constabulary" was set up.

Daniel O'Connell had organized the Catholic Association, which sought and achieved Catholic emancipation through Sir Robert Peel and the Duke of Wellington. Nevertheless, resistance to change was strong, and the implementation of the act was very slow. By 1886, for example, only twelve hundred justices of the peace of a total of five thousand were Catholics. The significance of O'Connell, though, is greater than this political achievement. By helping to change the upper-middle-class Catholic movement into a popular one, featuring clergy and peasantry, he finally and indissolubly cemented together the Catholic Church and Irish nationalism.

The period from 1845 to 1855 saw a profound change in the face of Ireland. During the first four years, about one million people died of disease and starvation; another two million emigrated, most of them to the United States. These "lucky" ones took with them a hatred for Britain fanned to a fever pitch by the great famine of 1847, in which at least a half-million Irish people died of starvation. The cause of the famine was the failure of the potato crop — their main food — and while Britain obviously could not be held responsible for the actual famine, many nevertheless believed that the magnitude of its consequences could have been considerably lessened if the British government had made more help available more quickly. One indirect effect of the famine was to further divide Ulster from the rest of Ireland. People to the north were much less dependent on agriculture than their southern countrymen. They had started a number of industries that were steadily expanding and providing increased wealth in the community. Thus, the impact of the famine was somewhat reduced, and Ulstermen did not share to the same degree the general Irish anger toward Britain.

The election of William Gladstone as British prime minister in 1868, with his famous declaration "My mission is to pacify Ireland," marks another milestone in Irish history. His conversion to the cause of Irish home rule is one of the more remarkable changes that has taken place in modern political history. Yet the actions he took in his first term of office indicate that he thought even then that the basis of the union was insecure, as it has proved to be.

In 1868, Gladstone removed one of the major Irish Catholic grievances when he disestablished the Church of Ireland in the face of strong conservative opposition in Britain. His opponents claimed — correctly, as it turned out — that such a move would undermine both British and Protestant control in that country. Yet the move was logically defensible. The 1861 census showed that 78 percent of the population was Catholic, 12 percent Anglican, and 9 percent Presbyterian. And although 70 percent of the Anglicans were in Ulster, even there they constituted a minority. The other main item of Irish legislation in Gladstone's first ministry was the Land Act of 1870, which gave tenant farmers greater security and more clearly defined rights. These had been actively sought since the formation of tenant associations immediately after the famine. The real significance of this act, however, was that it indicated a willingness on the part of the British government to start assuming some of its social responsibilities in Ireland.

The creation of the Home Rule League in 1870 by Isaac Butt, the son of an Anglican minister, returned the whole question of constitutional reform to the forefront of political discussion. The league acted as a channel for Nationalist sentiment, and in 1874 fifty-nine Home Rulers, who resolved to act as an independent group, were returned to Westminster. Gladstone attempted to lower the political temperature by introducing in 1881 a second land act designed to strengthen the tenant rights of the Irish peasantry; but this failed. In 1885, eighty-six home rule members (including some of the above) were returned to office, and together they held the balance of Brit-

23

ish legislative power. In return for their parliamentary support, Gladstone introduced the first of his three home-rule bills. In each of these bills the concept of Irish independence was strictly limited by the overall supremacy of the Westminster Parliament. What was envisioned by the concept of home rule was little more than glorified local government. Why then were passions so easily aroused? The answer is that everyone thought his or her own particular vested interest was being threatened.

The reasons for English opposition were economic and nationalistic. Ireland was a prime market for English goods and an important source of food supplies, both of which might be threatened by home rule. Even more important, conservative England saw in the move a challenge to its territorial integrity. Greeks, Italians, Australians, and Canadians should be, and indeed were, encouraged to manage their own affairs. But no recalcitrant group at home could be allowed to call into question the dominance of England or upset the status quo. So when Lord Randolph Churchill told the people of Larne that "Ulster will fight [against home rule] and Ulster will be right," and when he told the people in Belfast's Ulster Hall that there were many in England who would stand with them regardless of the consequences, he was voicing the opposition of the majority at the time. In Ulster the opposition was political, religious, and economic. First, the people considered themselves British because of their heritage, and they were unwilling to surrender that privilege. Second, they saw in the organization and policy of the home rule movement an identity between Catholicism and nationalism which to them justified the slogan "home rule is Rome rule." Finally, they felt — probably correctly — that any break with Britain would seriously undermine their industries, whose output was directed toward British markets, not Irish ones.

Under the influence of Charles Stewart Parnell, who succeeded Butt and led the Irish M.P.s at Westminster, the rest of Ireland was initially prepared to accept limited autonomy as a realistic step toward independence. Parnell managed on the one hand to persuade the English Liberals to propose limited autonomy and on the other hand to convince his Nationalist colleagues that it was desirable — a

24

considerable accomplishment. After his death in 1891, however, re-publican sentiment, fed by the injustices and hatreds of the past, again boiled to the surface, and Ireland was determined to be free.

The first home rule bill was defeated in the House of Commons by a split in the Liberal party's ranks. (The very fact that it was debated at all caused serious disquiet in Ulster and resulted in a great revival of the Orange Order.) The second bill, passed by the Commons but defeated in the House of Lords, prompted twelve thousand Orangemen from northern constituencies to affirm their total — and, if necessary, violent — opposition to home rule. By 1912, which saw the introduction of the third bill, James Craig (later Lord Craigavon, first prime minister of Northern Ireland) and Sir Edward Carson, the two leaders of Ulster unionism, were prepared for any eventuality. A provisional Ulster government was established, ready to begin operating on the day that a home rule bill became law. And gunrunning took place to the north and the south, which the English seemed powerless to stop. On Ulster Day, Sunday, September 28, 1912, after morning religious services, 471,414 Ulster men and women signed a solemn covenant against home rule. Subsequently, the Ulster Volunteer Force (UVF), made up exclusively of those who had signed the covenant, began to drill and march openly in the north in preparation for the expected battle.

In the rest of Ireland, two groups competed for public loyalty. The Irish Nationalist party in Westminster, now under the leadership of John Redmond, was still striving for home rule by constitutional means. The second group, started in 1906 and led by Arthur Griffith, was called Sinn Fein ("ourselves alone"). It held that the union with England was illegal and that Irish M.P.s should withdraw from Westminster and set up an Irish parliament in Dublin. While its influence was not immediately felt, it was certainly responsible, at least in part, for organizing the Irish Volunteers, who became the southern counterpart of the UVF. There was much support in England for the Unionists, especially in the Conservative party, and even British statesmen made speeches with violent overtones. Bonar Law, for example, publicly supported the Ulster

Volunteers; in 1912 he told a rally in England that he could imagine no lengths of resistance to which Ulster might go that he and, in his belief, an overwhelming majority of the British people would not be prepared to support.

The House of Lords delayed final passage of the bill from 1912 to 1914, during which time Prime Minister Asquith and the king considered excluding Ulster from the bill; but Redmond stoutly resisted. Due to the imminence of war, the act, once passed, was immediately suspended with the agreement of Redmond, Craig, and Carson, who all thought that the conflict with Germany was of more immediate concern. Republican elements in Ireland, however, viewed the war as an ideal opportunity to strike for independence while England was otherwise engaged. Thus, on Easter Monday, 1916, with little public support, Patrick Pearse, James Connolly, and Joseph Plunkett led an uprising in Dublin, and from the captured general post office declared Ireland a republic. The rebellion failed, many were hurt in the ensuing skirmishes, and hundreds were arrested. Most of the leaders were tried and executed, though one of them, Eamon De Valera, later to be president, was merely imprisoned; he had influential American friends who exerted pressure on the British government on his behalf. To the British, the uprising was simply an act of treason that had to be dealt with promptly and ruthlessly. To the Irish, it was an act of inspiration: not even its romantic absurdity could quench the spark of hope and anticipation that it ignited. James Connolly said, "Never had man or woman a grander cause; never was a cause more grandly served." And despite the cause's magnificent failure, many Irishmen began to agree with him.

In the two years following the Anglo-German war, attitudes in the north and the south hardened still further. Those in the north contrasted their military service in the armed forces with the treasonable actions of Sinn Fein and renewed their anti–home rule vows. In the south, Arthur Griffith and Michael Collins trained and organized anti-British terrorists, while De Valera went on a propagandizing and fund-raising trip to America. The pressure of violence finally led the British government to declare illegal both

Sinn Fein and the "Irish government" meeting in Dublin. The latter was formed by the seventy-three Sinn Fein candidates who were elected to Westminster in the 1918 election but refused to take their seats there.

The upshot of all this was "the troubles." The Irish Republican Army (IRA), the military wing of Sinn Fein, began a sustained campaign against the police and government troops. These latter, the Black and Tans, were a special force of British ex-servicemen who owed their name to the black belts and khaki uniforms they wore. This savage guerrilla war, which raged from 1920 to 1922, was characterized by atrocities and reprisals on both sides. In Ulster alone, nearly three hundred people were killed, many of them in Belfast. At the same time, there was considerable pressure on both sides to find an acceptable end to the conflict. Foreign opinion, especially that of Americans, was strongly against the British, who to them appeared to be coercing a people seeking self-determination. But the IRA also had its problems. Even after its policy was formally adopted by De Valera on behalf of the Dial (Irish parliament) in 1921, it still suffered from all the characteristic difficulties of insurgent groups: lack of money, ammunition, and manpower. Thus, the situation was a stalemate. Britain could win the war militarily, but to do so would mean abandoning political influence. The IRA could not win militarily but had the support of the people.

The solution, a compromise, came in two parts. In 1920, the Government of Ireland Act provided for two Irish parliaments: the one in Belfast was to govern Antrim, Down, Tyrone, Fermanagh, Armagh, and Londonderry; the parliament in Dublin was to govern the rest of the country. The authority of the northern parliament, which was opened by George V, was initially rejected by Ulster's Catholic population. To suspicious Unionist minds this indicated collusion with the terrorists of the south, and the new province got off to a bad start from which it has never recovered. In the south, all the elected Sinn Fein members boycotted the Dublin parliament, and eventually independence negotiations started between Lloyd George of England and Arthur Griffith and Michael Collins of Ireland. The resulting treaty, signed on December 6, 1921, gave Ireland independent dominion status within the British Commonwealth. In fact, it was similar to the Home Rule Act of 1914. The treaty included three provisions, however, which the Irish found distasteful and on which De Valera based his opposition to it. These provisions were an oath of allegiance to the British crown as befitted Commonwealth subjects, the freedom of Northern Ireland to withdraw from the newly created state and remain within the United Kingdom, and the retention by Britain of certain Irish naval bases. The treaty was finally approved by the Dial, and a provisional government under Michael Collins was set up in January 1922. Perhaps it is a commentary on the strength of Nationalist feeling on both sides of the Irish Sea that within a year of the treaty signing, Lloyd George was out of office, Griffith had died, and Collins had been murdered.

Since 1921

The division of Ireland became the main bone of contention in both the north and the south once the two governments took office. Although the election in June 1922 produced in Dublin a pro-treaty majority, the country was deeply divided on the treaty, and a form of civil war broke out soon afterward. The new government took over the anti-IRA role that had been relinquished by the British, while political opposition to the settlement was led by De Valera. However, the IRA commanded less and less support among the people, and De Valera finally announced the end of resistance in 1923. Intermittent violence continued, but it became even more isolated when De Valera and his followers took the oath of allegiance and assumed their place in the Dial in 1927. By this time, Collins had been succeeded by W. T. Cosgrave, whose administration laid the foundation of Ireland's political philosophy, one that remains substantially unaltered to this day. Politically, the country has sought to emphasize its sovereign independence, including its desire to see a united Ireland. Successive governments have tried to support an attractive and diversified industrial policy so that the country might attain both greater wealth and a greater degree of economic independence from Britain. Culturally, Ireland has stressed its "Irishness."

De Valera, who was prime minister from 1932 to 1948, continued these general policies but did not feel bound by the provisions of the treaty he had opposed. Early in his administration he abolished the oath of allegiance and during the period from 1936 to 1938 produced a new constitution that made the country a republic in everything but name. In fact, the degree of separation from Britain was underscored by the neutral stance that his government took during World War II. J. A. Costello, who followed him in 1948, completed the separation by proclaiming Ireland a republic on Easter Monday, 1949. In that same year, Westminster passed the Ireland Act, which established two constitutional points of great importance. The first was that the constitutional position of Northern Ireland could not be changed without the consent of the Northern Ireland Parliament at Stormont. (Now this is usually expressed in the phrase "without the consent of the majority.") The second was that the imperial government could not intervene in Ulster's internal affairs unless a breakdown in law and order occurred. This was the basis of the Downing Street Declaration of August 1969, which dispatched British troops to quell the Belfast riots.

In Ulster, Craigavon quickly accepted partition as the salvation of Northern Ireland, and Unionists pointed to the civil war in the south to illustrate their completely different attitudes toward Britain. Belfast's policy was to increase its British links and to maintain the Protestant ascendancy by whatever means necessary. Craigavon, who governed until 1940, said in 1934: "I have always said I am an Orangeman first and a politician and a member of this parliament afterwards. . . . All I boast is that we are a Protestant parliament and a Protestant State." And Craigavon's successor, Sir Basil Brooke (later Lord Brookeborough), who was prime minister until 1963, urged, "There are a great number of Protestants and Orangemen who employ Roman Catholics. . . . I would appeal to loyalists, whenever possible, to employ good Protestant lads and lassies." Eight months later, referring to this statement, he said, "Thinking out the whole question carefully . . . I recommend those people who are loyalists not to employ Roman Catholics, ninety-nine percent of whom are disloyal."

Terence O'Neill followed Brooke as Ulster's prime minister. Although he was from a background similar to that of his predecessor, he at least tried to establish a working relationship with the south. To this end he met with Sean Lemass, the Irish prime minister, in both Belfast and Dublin during 1965. These meetings took place at a time of reduced tension both between the north and the south — after the abortive IRA terrorist campaign of the 1950s had ended — and between the two communities in Northern Ireland. Nevertheless, the meetings immediately provoked protest. Right-wing Unionists interpreted them as the beginning of a rapprochement that would eventually undermine their monopoly of power. Catholics, though always pleased to have increased goodwill, really wanted substantial reforms and saw in the talks a chance to achieve them.

Early opposition to the more liberal attitudes introduced by O'Neill was spearheaded by an evangelical minister, Reverend Ian R. K. Paisley. He construed the government's policies in religious terms as a move toward an accommodation with Roman Catholicism, and in political terms as a betrayal of the province's historical heritage; thus he acted as a vociferous spokesman for many Protestants. His threat to lead his followers into the Catholic Divis Street area of Belfast to remove a tricolor (the Irish flag, whose display was illegal in Northern Ireland) flying above the republicans' headquarters during the election campaign of 1964 forced the home affairs minister at Stormont to order the police to do the job instead. The republicans and their sympathizers reacted violently, and the ensuing riots had a significance far beyond the immediate threat to life and property. First, because they took place during an election campaign, they were given immense press and television coverage all over the world. People were thus forcibly reminded of the undercurrents of bitterness that are an integral part of Ulster society. Second, the violence redivided that society into two antagonistic camps with a rigidity that had been missing since the early days of the province. Third, the riots signaled the beginning of the end of uninterrupted Unionist dominance. After this, people started to make their own voices heard through spokesmen for new political and special-interest groups. It was almost as if they were claiming that all the major political parties were irrelevant at the grassroots level.

Two of these new groupings were the Ulster Volunteer Force (UVF) and the Civil Rights Association (CRA). The former was an extreme right-wing Protestant group, which declared war on the IRA in the summer of 1966. After four Catholics were shot by its members on Malvern Street in 1968, O'Neill placed the UVF alongside the IRA on the outlawed list. This, of course, further outraged loyalist Protestants. The Civil Rights Association was organized in February 1967 with five objectives:

(1) to define the basic rights of all citizens;
(2) to protect the rights of the individual;
(3) to highlight all possible abuses of power;
(4) to demand guarantees for freedom of speech, assembly, and association;
(5) to inform the public of their lawful rights.

Such worthy intentions initially drew support from both Protestants and Catholics. But by 1968 these principles had been translated into a much more practical form. The civil rights movement was by then pursuing, more militantly, such demands as universal franchise at the local level, the redrawing of local election boundaries, legislation to outlaw discrimination in local government, a more equitable system for the allocation of council houses, and the repeal of the Special Powers Act. The particular stigma of the latter was that it included the right of the government to intern people without trial. To most Protestants these pursuits suggested that the CRA had abandoned its democratic ideals and had descended into a position of partisanship in the religio-political warfare. They believed that this program was in effect challenging

31

the very existence of the state by trying to change the well-tried formulas of government. Before long, the CRA had become largely Catholic, and its associations with People's Democracy, a radical student group based at Queen's University that kept steady pressure on Stormont with demands and demonstrations, further alienated conservative Unionists.

The inevitable clashes began between the conservative Unionists, radical Nationalists, and the police. The two worst took place in Derry in October 1968, when police clashed with CRA marchers, and at Burntollet in January 1969, when all four parties were involved and the CRA marchers brutally beaten. In fact, the violent behavior of the police in Derry is thought by some observers to be the incident that started the deterioration in law and order that finally led to the downfall of O'Neill's government. Also, at about that time Paisley was sent to jail for his part in an assault on news media personnel in Armagh during the previous November.

In April, Bernadette Devlin, a twenty-two-year-old radical student and a leader of the CRA, won a by-election to the United Kingdom parliament in London. By making a pungent speech on behalf of "the minority" only minutes after being sworn in at Westminster, Devlin gave worldwide exposure to Catholic demands for civil rights. One week later, O'Neill, having lost Unionist support, resigned and was succeeded by his distant cousin Chichester-Clark. The latter continued the policies of reform and on May 6 ordered all prosecutions against civil rights leaders and militant Protestants dropped in an attempt to improve community feeling.

The Orange celebrations on July 12, 1969, were marked by passionate outbursts in both speech and action. At Castlereagh, Paisley told assembled Orangemen that they were engaged in "the great battle of Biblical Protestantism against popery." At Moneymore, the prime minister depicted Irish republicans as murderers. And rioting occurred in the streets of Belfast, Lurgan, Derry, and Dungiven. By early August, Paisleyites, Nationalists, and police were clashing with greater violence and an increasing disregard for life and property. Finally, the Apprentice Boys' march and actions in Derry on August 12 so provoked that city's Catholics/Nationalist population that they attacked the marchers and later the police. Two days of bloody warfare followed before the police were able to "retake" the Bogside area in which the Nationalists had barricaded themselves. People everywhere in the province were terrified, intimidated, and vulnerable to attack, and Northern Ireland was on the verge of civil war.

It can be said that civil war started in Belfast on August 14. That night, extremists of both sides and B-specials, an auxiliary — largely Protestant — police force, went on a spree of shooting and arson that claimed eight lives. The spectacle of Bombay Street, between the Protestant Shankhill Road and the Catholic Falls Road, burning from end to end, signaled the total inability of the parliament at Stormont to enforce law and order and to protect the citizenry. Consequently, the British government had to step in, and Prime Minister Wilson sent six thousand soldiers into West Belfast to restore order. Thus, Britain, after a physical absence of less than fifty years, was again directly involved in the affairs of Ireland.

Since 1969

Over the past three decades, the British government has tried to keep in balance a two-pronged approach to Northern Ireland. On the one hand, the government has maintained a hard-line policy with regard to the insurgency of the Irish Republican Army. In view of the patent failure of local and regional security forces to keep the peace, Britain has had to employ its own troops in its own nation, both as peacekeepers and as a retaliatory force against a guerrilla force. On the other hand, Britain has tried to negotiate (sometimes over the heads of the Loyalists) with responsible representatives of the Nationalist community. This two-sided policy has had both advantages (Britain was the legitimate state against the terrorists) and disadvantages (Britain could not move toward Nationalist wishes any faster than Loyalists would allow it).

During the 1970s and 1980s, Ulster society was racked by a

loss of confidence unknown in prior years. While something like normal life carried on for most people, violence — or the threat of violence — was a constant part of their lives. People went to work or school just like other citizens in other parts of Britain. But they did so with the very real possibility of violence erupting around them. Very nearly every person in Ulster who came of age between 1970 and 1995 can attest to the reality of "the troubles." The number of Ulster's citizens maimed and killed can be documented, but another way of stating the reality is this: statistically, nearly every adult in Northern Ireland knew someone — from family neighborhood or workplace — who had been a victim of sectarian violence.

The 1970s was a particularly dark decade. During that period a majority of the deaths attributed directly to the troubles occurred. It seemed to many people that "atrocity" was a word that had been exhausted of meaning until another episode occurred that extended or deepened the definition. The chart below shows the number of deaths attributed to the troubles during the twenty-year period after 1969.

Annual Deaths (during twenty years of "the troubles")

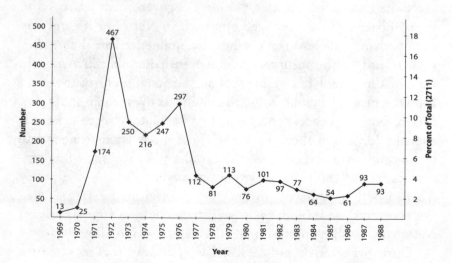

34

A statistical rendering like this is both unreal and very real — a chilling index of what went wrong in Northern Ireland during those years. A quarter of all the deaths in this period occurred during the first four years, and 61 percent occurred in the five-year period from 1971 to 1976. As we look back on that period, the wonder is not that some people broke down under the strain; the wonder is that most people were able to continue some semblance of normal life. That is, in fact, the story that most of the people of Ulster would like readers to know about them and their lives during the time of the troubles: they survived. It was not easy or pleasant; but with God's grace and their fortitude, they survived: babies were born, gardens were planted, pints of ale were hoisted, hymns were sung. Somehow, life went on.

The two communities — Catholic/Nationalist and Protestant/Loyalist — experienced the troubles in different ways. The violence seen and experienced by the Catholic community came from two sources: the security forces seemed to target their areas, and their community was invaded by Loyalist terrorists who set off small bombs or gunned down targeted individuals. But the violence seen and experienced by the Protestant community was mostly the darkly spectacular work of the IRA. Their bombs got the media coverage, as one might understand; the Protestant/Loyalist method of killing was more typically a single bullet. This caused a distortion in the public perception of violence in the 1970s and 1980s.

The spectacular episodes are those the media chose to feature, so they are the ones we tend to remember. There were so many in those years that to single some out is already to make an unfortunate choice. But some do stand out in memory:

- *Bloody Sunday* (1972). A Civil Rights Association protest march in Derry and subsequent confrontation with security forces resulted in British paratroopers firing at civilians. Four Catholics were killed.
- *Assassinations* (1976-79). The IRA targeted prominent members of the British political establishment: Christopher Ewart-Biggs, ambassador to Ireland, was killed in Dublin; Airey

Neave, Conservative Party spokesman on Northern Ireland, was killed in London; Richard Sykes, ambassador to the Netherlands, was killed in The Hague; Lord Mountbatten, cousin to the queen, was killed while sailing off the Irish Coast.

- *Hunger Strikes* (1981). Ten IRA prisoners starved to death in much-publicized hunger strikes. The first, Bobby Sands, is best known. His memory is revered in the Catholic/Nationalist community.
- *Harrod's* (1983). The IRA took its bombing campaign to England. A bomb killed six people while they were doing holiday shopping in London's premier department store.
- *Margaret Thatcher* (1984). The IRA bombed the hotel in which the Conservative party is holding its annual conference. Prime Minister Thatcher escaped without injury, but five other people were killed.
- *Enniskillen* (1987). The IRA bombed the ceremony at a war memorial on Remembrance Day (November 11) and killed eleven civilians, most notably Marie Wilson (whose father became a national figure because of his graceful response).
- *Downing Street* (1991). In the midst of the Gulf War, the IRA launched a mortar attack from Whitehall, London, on the residence of British Prime Minister John Major. Fortunately, he was uninjured.

The British government, along with its now-staunch ally in the Republic of Ireland, was willing to try several expedients to curb violence and to seek a political solution. Early in the troubles, the British seemed overwhelmed by the security problems, which is understandable, in view of the murder count from 1970 to 1976. British soldiers were deployed in the hope that a massive show of force would crush the violence and curb its public support. Along with a large military presence, the British government instituted a novel procedure of internment without trial. The legal argument was that jury trials, in the tradition of Anglo-Saxon common law, could not be relied upon in such extreme circumstances, and that internment based on the testimony of security officers was the only way to deal

36

with terrorists. The prison population in Northern Ireland swelled by 1980. Given the ambiguous legal status of such prisoners, there was a question of whether they should be allowed to claim political status — a sort of POW status — or be regarded as common criminals. Several leaders of British government had different views on this, and by 1980 there were alleged terrorists in prisons under both status arrangements. The new Conservative government under Margaret Thatcher refused to renew political status, and that refusal became the defining test of wills between London and the IRA. The prime minister would not yield, and ten men, led by Bobby Sands, committed suicide by starvation.

The British government, however, was always aware that force alone could not bring peace and that the way forward had to involve negotiations with the perpetrators of violence. There were able representatives of London on the scene, and behind the scenes, during the 1980s. Tom King, Sir Brian Mawhinney, and Sir Patrick Mayhew were particularly effective in both public and private ways, and they deserve much credit for their efforts to establish peaceful contacts during Northern Ireland's darkest years. They began a political process that was to accelerate in the 1990s and that would move quickly after the change of political climate in Eire, America, Britain, and Ulster after 1995.

By the mid-1990s a number of initiatives were apparently beginning to bear fruit. The British government reiterated its policy that the constitutional future of Ulster was in the hands of the people there, and that it would not contest an end to the British connection if a majority decided in favor of that. Moreover, the government openly invited Sinn Fein and its friends in the IRA to enter the political process and to join the discussions about peace. In reply, the IRA announced a cease-fire in 1994; that announcement was matched by the same from most of the Loyalist paramilitary groups. The British government kept the momentum going by ending its ban on direct public talks with paramilitary groups, and thus began the first public talks between British authorities and Sinn Fein since 1924.

After that, events began to move toward peace talks, but not without some confusion, some apparent contradictions, and some violent twists and turns. American president Bill Clinton, with the full approval of both Irish and British authorities, sent George Mitchell to Ireland to begin the last push that would culminate in a peace agreement. In 1995 Senator Mitchell seemed to be making progress. But the British government under John Major seemed to be putting obstacles in the way of progress. In any case, the IRA gave up on the peace process in a dramatic way with two spectacular bombings in 1996: in January, London was the target; in June, Manchester. The peace process was begun again after the election of a new government in Britain. The new prime minister, Tony Blair, quickly signaled his cooperation with the Clinton-Mitchell initiative. By mid 1997 the IRA announced, in a historic breakthrough, its "unequivocal" cease-fire, which paved the way for Sinn Fein to rejoin the peace talks.

When the final framework for peace was agreed to by all parties on Good Friday, 1998, the people of Northern Ireland were joined in rejoicing by people in many other nations. A breakthrough had been made that many had long hoped for but few had thought politically possible.

The public heroes of the negotiations deserve great credit, and some of them have since received considerable praise and tribute. David Trimble of the Ulster Unionist Party (the main Protestant loyalist party) joined John Hume of the Social Democratic and Labor Party (the main Catholic nationalist party) in sharing the Nobel Peace prize. Trimble should be further recognized as having the courage and political skill to join the talks and to marginalize — at least partly — the populist recalcitrance of Ian Paisley. Hume's political genius was to keep the talks going while working hard to encourage Gerry Adams of Sinn Fein to enter fully into the political process.

But the real heroes of the peace process were — and are — the people of Northern Ireland, the vast majority of whom came forward in great and small ways to declare their intention for peace. The politicians would agree: peace in Ulster was always meant for the people.

Situating Ourselves in the Conversation about Forgiveness

The narratives about three residential communities are the main concern of this book. But, before turning to those narratives, I propose to briefly review the growing body of literature on forgiveness and reconciliation. I believe this will provide important context for our later discussion of the Northern Irish situation. Since all commentators on Northern Ireland argue that religion is deeply imbedded in the fabric of conflict, it is clear that Christian people and institutions have a great deal for which to repent and a great need to seek and receive forgiveness. The ethics of forgiveness have long been at the heart of the Christian tradition. God, it seems, will go to any lengths to allow humans to see their hopeless condition. He provides a way for them to be forgiven and then reconciled to him and to each other. But the forgiveness often spoken about in religious terms is usually personal. Societal forgiveness and reconciliation are not usually what one thinks of when using those terms.

In recent years, however, there has been a revival of discussion about societal, even political, forgiveness. The classic work on the subject is by the late Hannah Arendt, the secular Jewish political theorist.[1] It was Arendt who noted the political impor-

1. Arendt, *The Human Condition: A Study of the Central Conditions Facing Modern Man* (Garden City, N.Y.: Doubleday, 1959).

tance of two "religious" traits, the ability to forgive and the ability to make promises. In our modern world, she argued, replete as it has been and is with conflict, oppression, and anxiety, the notions of forgiving (and being forgiven) and making promises (and receiving them) are of great political importance. The questions for places like Northern Ireland (and South Africa, Bosnia, and Rwanda), where religious-ethnic bitterness is so deep and long-standing, are these: Can there be any way out of all this? Can the cycle of retaliatory killings, of mutual acrimony and bitterness, of "un-Christian" behavior ever be reversed? Listen to Arendt's eloquent summary:

> The possible redemption from the predicament of irreversibility — of being unable to undo what one has done though one did not, and could not, have known what he was doing — is the faculty of forgiving. The remedy for unpredictability, for the chaotic uncertainty of the future, is contained in the faculty to make and keep promises. The two faculties belong together in so far as one of them, forgiving, serves to undo the deeds of the past, whose "sins" hang like Damocles' sword over every new generation; and the other, binding oneself through promises, serves to set up in the ocean of uncertainty, which the future is by definition, islands of security without which not even continuity, let alone durability of any kind, would be possible in relationships.[2]

The person who deserves the most credit for the renewed interest in Arendt is Donald W. Shriver, Jr., the noted American Presbyterian author and educator. His many accomplishments include having served as president of Union Theological Seminary. His book, *An Ethic for Enemies*, needs to be explored in some detail because it has helped shape the discourse on political forgiveness in general and the discussion on Northern Ireland in particular. While Shriver's main concerns turn on how Americans can be reconciled with wartime enemies — Germany and Japan — and

2. Arendt, *The Human Condition*, pp. 212-13.

with African Americans, we shall see that major academic colloquia have applied his analysis to the case of Northern Ireland.[3]

Shriver's work is moral, though not moralistic. It is based on an
empirical reality: that the twentieth century has been and contin-
ues to be devastating to humankind. Conflicts fueled by ethnic-
religious hatred continue. (As I write this, Serbian "ethnic cleans-
ing" has moved from Bosnia to Kosovo.) But the conflicts of this
century reach back a long way, as Shriver indicates in the moral
claim he makes: "We must do something about the memories and
the continuing legacies of the harms we have inflicted on each
other in the recent or remote past. . . . Absent forgiveness and its
twin, repentance, political humans remember the crimes of ancestors only to entertain the idea of repeating them."[4]

Just how forgiveness could or might work in politics follows
from Shriver's definition of political forgiveness. First, Shriver
says, political forgiveness begins with a collective memory "suf-
fused with moral judgment." He does not support the adage "forgive and forget." He believes that forgiveness is genuinely possible
only if we remember the injustice of an enemy and of the wrong
and injury done. There is always an element of moral evaluation in
a desire to forgive, because one forgives specific actions. One can
immediately see a difficulty that Shriver acknowledges, because
the willingness of an alleged perpetrator to receive forgiveness de-
pends on both parties agreeing on what needs to be forgiven.

Second, Shriver insists that forgiveness in politics does not require us to forsake the punishment of perpetrators. But Christians
must forego the vengeance that the first part of the definition
might engender. The third part of Shriver's definition goes along
with the forbearance emphasized in the second part — that is, one
must develop empathy for the humanity of the enemy. While
Shriver acknowledges that this is very difficult in deep, long-
standing conflicts in which much blood has been shed, he never-

---

3. Shriver, *An Ethic for Enemies: Forgiveness in Politics* (New York: Oxford
University Press, 1995).
4. Shriver, *An Ethic for Enemies*, p. 6.

theless rightly insists that without empathy for the former enemy's humanity, there is little hope for constructing a new and workable human community. Interestingly, Shriver is aware that one cannot push this process too far too fast, but must nurture it. Thus, the desire to make a new human community between "sinner and those sinned against" need not yet be called "reconciliation." That, he insightfully suggests, should wait until the end of the process which forgiveness begins.

Shriver's compelling analysis does not long stay in the abstract realm. Most of his work focuses specifically on three groups that mainstream America must come to terms with in its memories: the wartime enemies of Japan and Germany, and African Americans, to whom the larger culture still owes "that old and still unpaid debt." The rich texture of Shriver's work cannot be rehearsed here, but one story with a specific link to Ireland must be told. It is about St. Patrick, and how other communities can appropriate and be inspired by his story. This is particularly important in the case of Northern Ireland, where the two communities have cherished different heroes, have been empowered by different myths, and have seen no value in learning the stories of the other community.

The example involves the celebration of St. Patrick's Day, surely a day "owned" by Irish Americans. But two noted sociologists of African-American ethnicity, Nerys and Orlando Patterson, pointed out in the *New York Times* that St. Patrick's Day was as much for African Americans as Dr. King's birthday was for Irish Americans. Because greatness in any culture ennobles all cultures, the truly great stories are the property of all of us who seek a fully orbed humanity. For the Pattersons, the story of St. Patrick demonstrates that forgiveness can turn culture wars into transcendent possibilities. This former slave in Ireland escaped to England, embraced Christianity, and then embarked on a mission to Ireland. His goal was not only to convert his former slaveholders to Christianity but to encourage them to abandon the practice of slavery. For the Pattersons, St. Patrick is a transcultural hero. The conclusion of their article is memorable:

The historical St. Patrick also has an equally important lesson for African Americans and other minorities who feel they have been ill used. Violent abduction, slavery, hardship and terror did not lead him into ethnocentric hatred of the Irish. . . . This Patrick, who helped the Irish into the mainstream of Western history, who forgave and was forgiven, who suffered enslavement and overcame it, who epitomized the West's central drama — the outsider who stayed to transform the culture of his conqueror — belongs to us all.[5]

Those seeking further reflection on Shriver's book may want to consult the journal *Church and Society*, which recently devoted an entire issue to various analyses of *An Ethic for Enemies*.[6] Shriver himself is modest in his hopes for the impact his work will have outside the United States. He explicitly disavows the role of the pundit who offers prescriptions for other nations. Yet he does say, "That the politics of forgiveness has a place in every country's past and present I am certain; the daily news from Sarejevo, New Delhi, Belfast and Johannesburg is enough to convince anyone of that."[7]

But Shriver's book is having a greater impact than he thought it would. Both the daily news and *An Ethic for Enemies* seem to have convinced many people to inquire into the possibilities for forgiveness in politics in other than American locations. Among the most notable attempts to apply Shriver's insights is the series of colloquia held at the Woodstock Theological Center at Georgetown University in Washington, D.C.[8] The fact that the work of a leading Protestant theologian would be examined closely at a renowned Jesuit university suggests the ecumenical importance of

5. Nerys and Orlando Patterson, quoted by Shriver in *An Ethic for Enemies*, p. 231.

6. See the May/June 1998 issue of *Church and Society*.

7. Shriver, *An Ethic for Enemies*, p. 10.

8. The proceedings of these colloquia have been transcribed and printed and are available from the Woodstock Center, Georgetown University, Box 571137, Washington, D.C. 20057-1137.

Shriver's work, especially for the situation in Northern Ireland. In the pages that follow I will discuss the various contributions made at the three colloquia, the first held in 1995, the second in 1996, and the third in 1998. These were immensely important meetings at which Protestants and Catholics — scholars, activists, clergy, and laity — were able to talk freely. There was a remarkable degree of consensus both on the powerful political potential of forgiveness and on how long and difficult a road lay ahead before societal reconciliation would or could be achieved.

The first of the Woodstock meetings was held on November 15, 1995. Shriver presented some of the salient points in his book, and responses were given by two prominent Catholic intellectuals, Drew Christiansen of the U.S. Catholic Conference and J. Bryan Hehir of Harvard University. Christiansen affirmed that forgiveness and reconciliation have an important place in politics. But he suggested that while symbolic gestures by political or religious leaders are valuable in setting a tone for the forgiveness process, forgiveness is nevertheless personal and is known in the concrete realities of life. Hehir similarly affirmed that the social ethics of political forgiveness are consistent with the New Testament and desirable as practical politics. He offered a realist's caution, however, when he pointed out that punishment is necessary for war criminals, and that international law must enforce the Nuremberg precedent.[9]

The second Woodstock colloquium was held a year later, on December 9, 1996.[10] Assembled under the leadership of the Reverend James L. Connor, S.J., the director of the Center, along with some twenty-seven other participants, the colloquium asked directly if Donald Shriver's book was relevant to contemporary political conflicts. To focus the conversation, participants discussed the examples of Bosnia and Northern Ireland. (For present purposes, there is no need to deal with the discussions about Bosnia.)

9. *An Ethic for Enemies: A Forum with Donald Shriver*, Woodstock Center Colloquium, 15 November 1995.

10. *Forgiveness in Conflict Resolution: Reality and Utility*, Woodstock Center Colloquium, 6 December 1996.

A major presentation was given by the Reverend Brian D. Lennon, S.J., who is a founding member of the Interchurch Group on Faith and Politics in Portadown, Northern Ireland. He is an ecumenical leader in his city, which has been the scene of sectarian conflict over the Orange Order's marching through Nationalist neighborhoods, especially Drumcree. Lennon rightly enumerated the various ways in which ambivalence and anxiety characterize the situation in Northern Ireland. Both communities in Ulster are minorities — the Nationalists in Northern Ireland, the Unionists in the whole of Ireland. Both communities believe they cannot fully trust external governments. Nationalists can neither trust the word of the British government nor fully trust the government of Eire to represent them faithfully; the Unionists can neither trust the word or intentions of the Irish government nor trust that the British government will not make a deal with Dublin behind their backs. So, in this context of ambivalence and bitterness, what role can forgiveness play?

Lennon very valuably distinguished between forgiveness and reconciliation, and in doing so he seemed to agree with Donald Shriver: forgiveness begins the process of which reconciliation is the end; reconciliation must combine repentance and justice with forgiveness. Lennon wondered if Northern Ireland was at that time ready for major overtures of forgiveness. Yet, despite the odds against such overtures, he was able to see signs of hope both in terms of the new realities apparent (in late 1990) in the IRA and the Protestant paramilitaries, and in terms of shining examples of grace like that of Gordon Wilson, who forgave the IRA after his daughter, Marie, had died of wounds she suffered during the IRA bombing of Enniskillen on Remembrance Day, 1990. But Lennon's real hope lay in his pastoral insight that "at both a human and a spiritual level, our only way to freedom, to autonomy, and to recovery, as for all victims, lies through the often impossible task of forgiveness."[11]

Gerard F. Powers, a law professor at George Washington University and a foreign policy advisor to the U.S. Catholic Conference,

11. *Forgiveness in Conflict Resolution*, p. 58.

made the second presentation at the 1996 colloquium. Powers rehearsed the various historic reasons why forgiveness and reconciliation are necessary in Northern Ireland. In view of the power of memory to divide societies, he noted the positive role that some of the churches were beginning to play. In 1994, he pointed out, there were wonderful examples of bridge-building through statements of apology by the two primates. The Archbishop of Canterbury, Dr. George Carey, went to Christ Church cathedral in Dublin. There he preached on the scandal of the religious dimension of the Northern Irish troubles, and how that scandal pointed up the need for acts of forgiveness and reconciliation. He contributed to the healing process himself by stating forthrightly, "I am aware of just how much we English need to ask forgiveness for our often brutal domination and crass insensitivity in the eight hundred years of history of relationships with Ireland. . . . [To recognize] the follies, the evils and the atrocities committed in the name of whatever ideals we follow, is to begin to build the bridge."[12]

Later that year, Cardinal Cahal Daly, the Roman Catholic primate of Ireland, accepted Dr. Carey's invitation to preach at Canterbury Cathedral. Like Carey, he offered a plea for forgiveness, stressing the need to heal memories. He apologized and asked forgiveness for the wrongs and hurts inflicted by the Irish on the British, especially since the revival of the troubles in the late 1960s. Daly stressed that reciprocal forgiveness was necessary for healing religious and social relationships as well as political relationships in Northern Ireland.

Powers told these stories to laud the two bishops for their courage. But he also noted that the bishops' statements were not met with universal approval. As for George Carey, Nationalists in Ireland wondered if he spoke for very many British Protestants, especially those from Ulster. Unionists, on the other hand, cringed a bit at Carey's apparent presumption to speak for them on Irish matters; indeed, some Unionists wondered if there was any need for a British leader to apologize at all. As for Cahal Daly, the reverse was true.

12. *Forgiveness in Conflict Resolution*, p. 61.

Many Nationalists had felt the scourge of British discrimination but were themselves not supporters of the IRA (a majority of Catholics could be so described). Consequently, they disliked their bishop's declaring a kind of moral balancing between recent IRA terrorist activities and the many years of British rule in Ireland. Many Unionists, on the other hand, saw Daly as genuine but sadly unrepresentative of the feeling in the Nationalist community.

In the end, Powers said, Carey and Daley's statements and requests for forgiveness were to be welcomed. But, as he saw it, there were other pronouncements far more effective in beginning the forgiveness process: the statements made in the context of the Drumcree marches in Portadown in the summer of 1995. Both the Catholic Church and the governing committee of the Presbyterian Church issued a joint statement condemning Nationalist violence but placing special blame on Unionists for insisting on the marches that led to violence. Soon after, twenty-five Presbyterian clergy issued another statement asking forgiveness from God and from Catholics because "Presbyterians have been directly involved and . . . all of us, by association, have been tainted by this communal sin."[13] This kind of apology has been much more compelling because it is specific and more immediate than that of the archbishops.

Similar pleas for forgiveness and expressions of forgiveness have also been very effective, according to Powers. When former terrorists from either community have publicly repented of their violent acts and asked for forgiveness, it has touched people in a special way. And when families of the victims of violence have offered forgiveness to the perpetrators — even when the latter have not repented — the effect has been even more powerful. By highlighting these expressions, Powers did not intend to denigrate the public apologies of the religious leaders. He was merely pointing out that while cross-community bridge-building is necessary at the leadership level, the process of repentance, forgiveness, justice, and reconciliation is likely to have greater impact as it gets closer to the present and to immediate events and the people involved therein. In making this

13. *Forgiveness in Conflict Resolution*, p. 63.

distinction, Powers echoed a point made by Drew Christiansen: that the personal is political, and the political is personal.

The next major engagement with Donald Shriver's work also took place at the Woodstock Theological Center. The meeting, held on June 18, 1997, focused exclusively on Northern Ireland. Once again, Father James Connor, the director of the Woodstock Center, and Robert Hennemeyer, the "forgiveness" project director, assembled an excellent group of discussants: two British/Irish academics and three clergy from Northern Ireland. For our purposes I will focus on one of the academics and two of the clergy.

The most famous speaker — and probably the person all the participants wanted to hear — was Cardinal Cahal Daly. His comments were labeled "a Catholic view in the program proceedings." But, although his standpoint was clearly Catholic, his observations were in many ways ecumenical.

Cardinal Daly began with references to his and (Archbishop of Canterbury) George Carey's exchange of pulpits and the pleas for forgiveness that both had offered. For this occasion, he repeated what he had said at the Fitzroy Presbyterian Church in Belfast on November 26, 1995. This was an important inclusion, since his host at that church, the Reverend Ken Newell, was seated on the same platform with him at Georgetown.

> As I, a Catholic Pastor, address this mainly Protestant congregation, and recall the atrocities which we now name by the place where they happened, such as Whitecross, Darkley, Shankill Road, Enniskillen; and as I reflect that the perpetrators of these atrocities, though they would not listen to the pleas of their bishops and priests or follow the teaching of their church, were nevertheless "of us," I can only humbly ask forgiveness from you for such deeds.[14]

---

14. *Forgiveness in Conflict Resolution: The Northern Ireland Experience*, Woodstock Center Colloquium, 18 June 1998, p. 6. All subsequent references to this document will be cited parenthetically in the text.

To this catalogue of apologies he added the apology made by British Prime Minister Tony Blair early in 1998:

> That one million people should have died in what was then part of the richest and most powerful nation in the world is something that still causes pain as we reflect on it today. Those who governed in London at the time failed their people through standing by while a crop failure turned into a massive human tragedy. (p. 6)

While Daly acknowledged the value of such statements and requests for forgiveness, he echoed Gerard Powers's point that such requests would be more effective if they had come not so much from national religious and political leaders but from those formerly engaged in violence and conflict, or those closely associated with such persons or groups. He was particularly impressed, for example, by the statement of Gusty Spence, a former Loyalist paramilitary leader. In announcing the Loyalist cease-fire in October 1994, Spence also offered "the loved ones of all innocent victims over the past twenty-five years abject and true remorse." Daly courageously went on to comment, "Sadly, this loyalist declaration has never been reciprocated by the IRA or by any other republican paramilitary group. The ambiguities and evasions of Sinn Fein spokesmen where challenged about IRA atrocities have been, by contrast, shameful" (p. 7).

Daly then delineated what he believed would have to happen if true repentance was to occur: that those who were repentant would have to live truly amended lives. Further, if forgiveness was to be relevant and effective in politics, political relationships would have to change. It would be most effective if those offering apologies were also actively working with groups or communities to change the attitudes that had led to the wrong actions in the first place. It was vital, according to Daly, that Christians take the lead in changing attitudes, healing memories, and repenting of past wrongs: "The Christian will say that both the salvation of souls and the welfare of society are at stake. Extirpating hatred and vengeance is a matter of both spiritual salvation and the survival of democracy" (p. 8).

As Daly pointed out, perceptions are oftentimes more important than so-called realities. Indeed, one of the main sticking points between the two communities is the different perceptions they have about common events; further, each community remembers the other's offenses, but both communities seem to have largely forgotten how they have wronged each other. In this respect, Daly made a very astute observation that I had not previously heard: that cherishing and nurturing memories of past wrongs were more characteristic of a community insecure about its identity and afraid for its own future than of a community secure in its identity and confident about its future. Interestingly, the historic roles in this respect have been reversed in recent years. The Nationalist community, formerly relatively excluded and powerless, is now more confident than ever about its identity and future. The Unionist community, formerly relatively included and powerful, is now less confident than ever about its identity and future. Therefore, Daly suggested, the Catholic and Nationalist community must be particularly proactive in joining the Protestant and Unionist community in remembering their common past and in forgiving mutually and completely (p. 8).

Daly concluded his comments with affirming pleas for pardon and expressions of forgiveness, but noted that although these are necessary preludes to conflict resolution, they are not sufficient in and of themselves. The movement toward reconciliation will come only and fully when individuals have amended their lives and various structures and institutions have been altered to prevent the kinds of situations in which injustice has occurred (p. 9).

Paul Arthur, a professor of politics at the University of Ulster, was the next speaker. He candidly stated that his perspective was a secular one. For him the notion of forgiveness in politics was oxymoronic. But he did acknowledge that some way had to be found to change people's mind-set, whatever terms one chose to use. He cautioned that a peace agreement, while to be welcomed, is only part of the peace process. A peace agreement creates an opportunity, but the real work of peace-seeking only then begins (p. 12).

50

The analysis that Arthur provided was both original and insightful. Taking his assignment as the realist who looked at those things blocking societal reconciliation, he reminded his listeners that the study of politics is not first of all about political behavior but about special human traits: imagination and myth-making. Arthur quoted the literary critic Lionel Trilling to great effect: "Unless we insist that politics is imagination and mind, we will learn that imagination and mind are politics and of a kind that we will not like" (p. 17). Trying to imagine a new political life for Northern Ireland, therefore, would require all people of goodwill to overcome some significant obstacles to forgiveness: the problem of leadership, the question of memory, and the issue of victimhood.

The first obstacle is one whose makeup has recently changed. As Arthur noted, no one could have foreseen the shift in political leadership that has emerged in the past two years. What had been, and perhaps still might be, an obstacle to peace was that those in leadership — especially Unionists — were never sure that they could carry their membership with them. The political success of the fringe Unionist groups has, paradoxically, encouraged David Trimble, the leader of the largest Unionist party, the Ulster Unionist Party (UUP), to be more inclusive in his approach. Indeed, Trimble is to be the leader of the new Assembly under the terms of the Good Friday Agreement. In July 1998 he exercised considerable leadership in helping to diffuse the standoff at Drumcree. He has since received the Nobel Peace prize, shared with Catholic/Nationalist leader John Hume.

The second obstacle to reconciliation is community memory. On this subject, Arthur spoke autobiographically, having been raised a Catholic in the Bogside area of Derry. It is not memory itself (because that is vital to human well-being) but "the memory of wounds," he pointed out, that can be "one of our deadliest problems." Furthermore, the most evocative of these are the memories of the heroes who laid down their lives, most notably Wolfe Tore in 1798 and Patrick Pearse in 1916. Young people of today would add the name of Bobby Sands, the hunger-strike martyr of the early 1980s. The attachment of many people in the Nationalist community to the IRA turns on this sort of evocation of memory (p. 19).

The third obstacle to reconciliation, according to Arthur, is the issue of victimhood and the lack of empathy, both in Irish history and in contemporary Ulster. The Catholic and Nationalist community learned from the Protestant and Loyalist community — by either mobs or militia — that those who could intimidate and inflict violence would be the winners. Loyalists, for their part, cite various examples, from the massacres of Protestants in 1641 to the recent IRA bombing campaigns, to show that the Catholics have also been violent toward them. According to Arthur, this cycle of violence leads to "a political economy of helplessness, a victim-based society in which memories of past injustice and humiliation are so firmly entrenched in both communities and the sense of entrapment so complete that the hunger strikes are a metaphor for the entrapment of the larger society" (p. 22). The Catholics have enhanced their sense of victimhood with their own religious iconography. An example: graffiti artists in West Belfast portrayed a hunger striker being comforted by Mary and wrote under the image, "Blessed are those who hunger for justice." However, on the day that Bobby Sands died, the Anglican archbishop was burying a policeman murdered by the IRA. The archbishop asked, "Where does the real agony lie? Is it with those who use the threat of the choice of death or with those who have no choice?" (p. 23). This is the Protestant reply in this nexus of victimhood, in which Protestants feel so threatened in their daily lives in Northern Ireland that the noble deaths of those defending their culture seem to be made meaningless.

Arthur spoke persuasively, even movingly, about the realities that block the road to forgiveness and social reconciliation. In his conclusion, he pointed to hopeful signs that seem to augur well for potential breakthrough. Most importantly, the long-suffering ordinary people of Northern Ireland seem to have moved ahead of most of their leaders, both in believing that their futures can be different and in believing that they can have a hand in shaping those futures. People no longer so weighed down by fatalism can begin to *imagine* a different sort of politics and society for themselves and their children. Ordinary Protestants can say to their leaders in the Orange Order that they will not march anymore. Ordinary Catholics can say to their leaders in Sinn Fein that they will no longer cover up for the violent men in their community. With sentiments like these coming from the common people, political and religious leaders everywhere will find their way to the negotiating table.

In the end, Arthur believes that the way forward to peace and reconciliation must transcend historic points of origin of the wounded memories in both communities. Several people recently have spoken of many "acts of transcendence," which prefigure the society of grace and peace. For example, the poet Seamus Heaney, when receiving his Nobel prize, told of the massacre of nine workmen in Kingsmill. When they were told to line up, a gunman asked, "Are there any Catholics among you?" The one Catholic started to step forward, but his Protestant comrades stopped him, thinking that he was being singled out to be killed. In fact, it was an IRA ambush, and the Catholic was saved and the nine Protestants killed. Another story comes from the other side. An IRA bomb that killed a number of policemen also killed a nun. In a historic overture, members of the Catholic community asked to attend the policemen's funerals. This was the first time that folk from the Nationalist community showed empathy for what happened to the police. Their act of transcendence established cross-community empathy that was to be long lasting (p. 26).

The third presenter at this meeting was — and is — a very important player in the interreligious dialogue about forgiveness in Northern Ireland: Reverend Ken Newell, pastor of the Fitzroy Presbyterian Church in Belfast. Fitzroy Church is a strategically important church both because it is in the university area and because it is one of the more important churches of evangelical persuasion within the Presbyterian Church of Ireland. For Ken Newell to be a leader in intercommunity reconciliation and for him to do that work from a conservative Presbyterian church is in itself a minor miracle. In his presentation he made four important points.

The profile of forgiveness is small but growing. Forgiveness, Newell began, does not have a high profile in the political life of Northern Ireland. It is rare to hear people confessing the wrongs that their own community has committed against the other community. Blaming the other community for wrongs it has committed is more typical in a society that has experienced a generation of violence and counterviolence. Yet there is a small but promising movement in most churches to examine the past and seek an honest way forward (p. 58).

When forgiveness begins, the impact is great. There are many individuals who, despite having experienced a great deal of suffering, have come forward to express their forgiveness in a way that has caused the whole community to admire their courage and grace. One such individual was the late Gordon Wilson, whose daughter, Marie, was killed by the IRA in the Enniskillen bombing. His words of forgiveness were broadcast so widely that the bombers must have heard them. Even the queen included his words in her Christmas address. He toured widely, telling of his loss and of the need for reconciliation. Ken Newell believes that Gordon Wilson is a "great icon of grace." His story must be kept alive as an antidote to the icons of death seen every day on the walls of Belfast. His story must be kept alive for future generations because, as Newell says, "in Gordon Wilson, Christ came back to Enniskillen" (pp. 58-59).

A climate of forgiveness cannot *spread until all parties address painful memories that cause distrust.* Only when all parties are able to share the painful memories and have them acknowledged by others will the cycle of hatred and violence be broken. For example, Newell said, the *Ne Temere* Decree on Mixed Marriages had left a permanent scar of bitterness in the Protestant community. Many Protestants believed that, because of the decree, their marriages were questioned, their children stigmatized, and even their Christian commitment put into a second-class category. In 1998 a Catholic bishop apologized for the hurt that *Ne Temere* had caused, and that single act sent a powerful message to the Protestant community that their bitter memories were at least acknowledged.

Newell went even further — and this took courage, given the fact that he was speaking in a Catholic setting. He noted that the pope had apologized to the Jewish community for the long tradition of anti-Semitism in the Catholic Church. His holiness said that such attitudes were not part of the mind of Christ, and that it was time for the Catholic Church to say so. But Newell's dream was that one day the pope would sit down with a group of Protestant ministers from Northern Ireland "to find ways to say I am sorry to our community as he has to the Jews. His words would have a powerful effect in Northern Ireland, for he could release the anger, pain, and hurt that still surrounds these issues" (p. 62).

The only soil in which the plant of forgiveness can take root is the nurturing soil of contact between isolated persons, groups, and communities. In Northern Ireland, like South Africa, the people ready to make apologies are those with long-standing contact with members of the other community. While perhaps an obvious point, it bears repeating: Contact between people is a vital first step toward peace. Ken Newell gave an astonishing example. From 1990 to 1993 he met with a multidenominational clergy group at Clonard Monastery in Belfast to talk with the leadership of Sinn Fein. As the participants became acquainted, they came to know each other's stories, to acknowledge the wrongs and hurts that had been inflicted on each other's communities, and even to say "I'm sorry" for them. Gerry Adams, the leader of Sinn Fein, once admitted, "I genuinely regret every young English soldier who goes back to Britain in a coffin" (p. 63). Newell has encouraged Adams to express that sentiment publicly, but understands that Adams is under political constraint. Yet many hearts long to see the political impact of such a public disclosure.

Newell concluded with a plea for understanding and friendship in explicitly Christian terms. In it one hears the echo of evangelical sincerity and earnestness:

Before we can say [we're] sorry to each other and ask and receive forgiveness, we have to meet, communicate, listen, and become friends. It is as friends, as brothers and sisters in Christ, that we

55

can become agents in the hands of God for creating the kind of society in Northern Ireland where all feel valued and where our future is in stark contrast to our painful past. It is already happening. The darkness is breaking up, and the signs of a new dawn are all around us. (p. 64)

I hope this discussion has helped to situate us in the conversation about the meaning and the context of forgiveness in the Northern Ireland situation. Ken Newell said it well when he commented that the darkness was breaking up in Northern Ireland. There have been, in truth, signs of a new dawn. Much of the new light has come out of the long twilight struggle for forgiveness, peace, and reconciliation by many people in many walks of life.

In my view, first among the long-term peacemakers are the members of three residential communities: the Corrymeela Community, the Christian Renewal Centre, and the Columbanus Community of Reconciliation. While the three communities operate in slightly different ways, they are generally quite similar in what they do. In the first place, the mere fact that such ecumenical residential communities exist in a divided society is already a statement for peace. The members of the communities staff the residences, and they act as hosts to visitors. All three communities have full programs of lectures, workshops, and retreats. These busy places might, in any given month, conduct a series of lectures about forgiveness in politics, sponsor a weekend retreat for teenagers brought from both Catholic and Protestant schools, and hold an interreligious prayer vigil. Behind the scenes they also use their credibility to bring together for talks political people who would not, or could not, acknowledge each other in public. The communities also have a presence on the airwaves: all regularly take part in the religious programming of the BBC. In short, these three communities have a deep and broad impact in Ulster society. It is to their stories that we now turn.

The Corrymeela Community

The Corrymeela Community has two physical locations, near Ballycastle in county Antrim and in Belfast. While the urban part of community life is important to the work of Corrymeela, it is the site near Ballycastle that most people envision when they think of Corrymeela.

The complex of buildings at the edge of a cliff overlooking the northeast coast is dominated by a large white building. The entire complex is called "Corrymeela," but it is this white building that all visitors remember. I have walked along the sea road, past the golf course, toward Corrymeela in the months of January, May, June, and September. Whatever the weather — from sun and warm breezes to slatting rain and cutting wind — the visitor is unprepared, when rounding the last turn, for the beauty and grandeur of the place. The visitor need not remind himself that this is a place of peace; the setting tells it, and the Irish-Gaelic name for Corrymeela is "Hill of Harmony." But, at the same time, the visitor must remind himself that this haven of peace, so much appreciated, is necessary because of the bitter violence in Belfast, only about fifty miles away. This is the paradox that Corrymeela both symbolizes and tries to address: that in Northern Ireland one finds wonderfully kind and thoughtful Christian people living and working in one of the loveliest physical locations in Europe; but also that in the same country, from 1969 to 1998, one witnessed the

57

worst scenes of fighting in Western Europe since the end of World War II.[1]

Corrymeela is, of course, much more than a place. It is an idea, and, above all, it is people. The idea that empowers the vision of Corrymeela is that Christians can make a difference in the world, and that Christian community is the model for that difference. The vision of Corrymeela is in self-conscious continuity with the work of Francis of Assisi, Patrick of Ireland, and Columba of Derry and Iona. As John Morrow writes, looking backward over thirty years, "From the beginning there was always a deep sense of affinity with his [Francis's] strong affirmation of all God's creation, his love for the poor and his spirit of gentleness, forgiveness and peace."[2]

The place and the vision, however, are best seen and known through the people of Corrymeela Community. In the next few pages, we'll spend some time getting to know Ray Davey, the founding father of Corrymeela and the motivating force behind its success. Davey, one of the saintliest and yet most down-to-earth men most people have ever met, would object to this emphasis on him. He would point us to the scores of other people vital to the work done on the Hill of Harmony and in Belfast. He would think of the people who kept everything operating, like Billy McAllister and Kathleen Bakewell; people vital to the programs, like Gerry Cassidy, Doug Baker, and Carmel Heaney; and people with special responsibilities for leadership, like John Morrow, Harold Good, Derek Wilson, Mike Earle, Alistair Kilgore, Colin Craig, and Trevor Williams.

1. Many books and articles have been written about the Corrymeela Community. This chapter draws upon the following works, to which readers wanting deeper knowledge of Corrymeela are referred: Ray Davey, *Take Away This Hate* (Belfast: Corrymeela Press, 1986); *A Channel of Peace: The Story of the Corrymeela Community* (London: Marshall Pickering, 1993); John Morrow, *Journey of Hope: Sources of the Corrymeela Vision* (Belfast: Corrymeela Press, 1995); and Alf McCreary, *Corrymeela: The Search for Peace* (Belfast: Christian Journals, 1975). This last book was reprinted in an American edition, with a new preface by the author, as *Corrymeela: Hill of Harmony in Northern Ireland* (New York: Hawthorn Books, 1976).

2. Morrow, *Journey of Hope*, p. 8.

But, in the end, Ray Davey is the person without whom Corrymeela would never have existed. Everyone accepts that fact even as our self-effacing "hero" is uncomfortable with heroic representations of him.

Ray Davey, a man whose demeanor and activity belie his octogenarian status, is — to use a trite phrase — a legend in his own time. All who come in contact with him comment on both the generosity of his spirit and the expansiveness of his vision. He is truly one of the great men in the history of Northern Ireland. He would be the one to say, however, that this extraordinary century made him what he became, and perhaps he would be right.

Born during World War I, Ray was the fourth child in a family that would have five children. His father, a clergyman in the Presbyterian Church of Ireland, lived and ministered in Dunmurray, near Belfast, during the years that Ray was growing up. His parents, Ray remembered later, were quite tolerant of his energies and gave him a lot of leeway in his formative years. While he was surely given a Christian upbringing, it was one in which imagination and energy were valued. Ray's faith matured gradually. Although he never had a dramatic "conversion experience," he believed he "knew" God through Christ in a very personal way. Moreover, this Christian faith was not about rules and regulations but about a way of life characterized by grace and peace.

Ray's education was conventional for a person of his social class. His school, the Academical Institution, and his university, Queen's, were the sorts of places that Presbyterian ministers' sons were expected to attend in the 1920s and 1930s. Ray graduated from Queen's University in 1936, in the depths of the Great Depression, when about a third of all people seeking work were unemployed. He had decided on a clergy career by then, so he was encouraged to attend Presbyterian College near Queen's campus. He completed his course of training in the customary three years, though one of those three years he spent in Edinburgh. By 1939 he was ready to be ordained into the ministry of the Presbyterian Church of Ireland. He would have been ordained and received his first clerical appointment in Bangor, but just then the war began — the war that would change his world, and him, forever.

Ray volunteered for duty with the troops as a worker with the YMCA. He left home in late September 1940 and arrived by ship at Port Said on New Year's Day 1941 for service in North Africa. After spending a period of time out in the desert, Ray was assigned to the YMCA Centre in Tobruk, a former Italian naval base at the east end of the Mediterranean. He would work and minister there until June 1942. He describes the impact of this assignment:

> That experience in the YMCA Centre in Tobruk has remained with me as a prototype of a meaningful Christian Community. It was located right at the place where life was lived in all its war-time pain, frustration and uncertainty. It was at the point where the need was the greatest, where so many young men from so many different countries were, in their suffering and sacrifice, paying the price that is demanded when the nations can find no other way of settling their conflicts. It seemed to me a blood sacrifice they were asked to pay for all the greed and pride of the most wealthy and cultured nations in the world.
>
> The Centre became a place where many came to unburden themselves, to talk about their hopes and fears, their sorrows and anxieties, the responsibilities they had to carry and the decisions they had to make. This Desert Community did fit into John Mackay of Princeton's description of the Christian community as "a place where life is lived most closely to man's need."[3]

In late 1942 Ray heard that there was a shortage of chaplains. He needed to be ordained, though, so his presbytery in Belfast made arrangements for his ordination by the Church of Scotland in Jerusalem. This was his personal situation when Rommel brought his brilliant methods of attack to Tobruk on June 20, 1942. For more than a year, Ray was a prisoner of the Italians in "Camp 70." In September 1943, the Italians capitulated in the

3. Quoted in *A Channel of Peace*, p. 34.

face of Allied advances, so the prisoners in the camps dreamed of release and return home. But their hopes were crushed by German efficiency: the German army took over the Italian camps and moved all the prisoners to Germany. Ray was transferred to Stalag 4A, a designation for a large group of work camps for prisoners of war in and around Dresden. Ray's duties were as "spiritual comforter" to the men in the eighty camps and two hospitals in the stalag. He was thus able to move around in a way that few other prisoners could, and he performed a great service counseling and encouraging the men.

By early 1945, Ray had been a prisoner of war for two-and-a-half years, and had been in service in the desert for two years prior to that. Away from home and comfortable surroundings for so long, he thought he had seen just about everything. There was, however, one more experience in Germany that would put his entire wartime service into focus: the firebombing of Dresden by British and American troops on February 14, 1945. Many people today forget that the bombing of Dresden was calculated to do as much damage as possible. The bombs used and the targets chosen were intended to create a new phenomenon, the firestorm. The other city bombed by the Allies in 1945, half a world away — Hiroshima — is remembered as the place where modern warfare reached its horrific apotheosis. In fact, however, the firestorm that engulfed Dresden was equally horrific, and the devastation equally intentional.

Ray had been in Dresden, working with the prisoners, on February 13. He wanted to stay because the need there was so great. But his German army guard insisted that Ray return to his assigned barracks in Hohnstein, some ten miles from Dresden. It seems that Ray's pass had expired! So he was spared the bombing — but not the sight or the memory of it. It is not clear even now how many people died in Dresden on February 14. Allied prisoners had been marched there because the Red Army was advancing from the east; in addition, many civilian refugees had flocked into the city to escape the Russians. The physical devastation of Dresden was horrific beyond belief, and it would forever mark this young

Irishman who made his way back into the city the following day to see if he could help.

Ray would return to Dresden in 1985, forty years later, for an anniversary service sponsored by the British and German councils of churches. Revisiting that city with his wife, Kathleen, was a moving experience. What he says about it helps us to see that none of his wartime experiences — not even his long imprisonment — left him bitter:

It was Rogation Sunday and Christof Ziemer asked if we would both take part in the service. Kathleen read one of the lessons and I was invited to explain why I had come back. I had nothing prepared and just spoke from the heart, telling the people how I felt. I explained that the last time I had been in their city I was a prisoner and an enemy. I told of the suffering and loss of many of my colleagues, and how some had died of exhaustion and exposure due to the forced marches. Then I went on to tell of the horror and outrage many of the prisoners had felt as they saw the terrible aftermath of the massive bombing. I ended what I had tried to express as follows: "But now today, at this Table, we all meet together to share this bread and this wine. In doing so we experience the Presence, the Forgiveness and the Healing of our One Lord and Master. 'For He is our peace and has broken down the dividing wall of hate and made us one people.'"

I knew then why I had wanted so much to come back, to be there with those people of Dresden, at the one table, with the One Christ. I also believe that I was speaking for a vast number of my fellow prisoners-of-war.

Later on our hosts took us to the famous Dresden Opera House, the Semper Oper. It had been very severely damaged in the raids and had just been re-opened a few weeks before on the 40th anniversary of the 1945 attacks. The same opera, Karl von Weber's *Der Freischutz*, was being played as on the fatal night.

During the interval, when the lights went up, a lady next to Kathleen began to talk to her. She explained how she and her husband had been at the service and recognized us. It had meant much to them both. They had come over from Munich, where they now lived, on a four-day visit. They decided to go to the *Kreuzkirche* because her husband had been confirmed there. At the time of the raids he was in the army, though he was only sixteen years old, and living away from home in barracks. During that night his mother, his six-year-old brother and both grandparents were killed. Ever since, he had been filled with hatred against the British and Americans, and vowed he would never forgive them. But that day at the service he felt, for the first time, that he could forgive.

Unfortunately at that point the theatre lights were dimmed as the opera continued. Then at the end in the rush we missed them and I felt very sad that I had not been able to talk to him. As we left the theatre, we were soon merged in a large crowd with many cars moving off. Suddenly a man appeared dodging through the traffic. He grasped me by the hand and, as I [grasped] his, I asked for his name. He replied that his name did not matter. He just wanted to shake my hand. He held it fast for a moment. I could see that there were tears in his eyes, and all he could say was, "Now I can forgive," and then he rushed away, to be lost in the crowds.

It was easy to use the word "forgiveness" at such a time. But what did it mean? Who forgives whom? It is so easy to get into a tit-for-tat situation. What about the bombing of London and Coventry? What, then, about Berlin and Hamburg? What about the Nazis and the concentration camps? But what about the Versailles Treaty and devastating reparations after World War I? There is only one place where we can go beyond the military and political arguments, and that is at the Table before the Cross of Christ. Here we meet on level ground. We recognize that we are all guilty, we are all in it together, both as nations and individuals. So the only prayer we can pray is "Father forgive — each one and all of us."[4]

4. *A Channel of Peace*, pp. 49-51.

In early May 1945, the Germans allowed the Allied prisoners to go free. Ray joined his excited friends as they made their way in search of the Americans. They promptly ran into the Red Army. But the Russians recognized them and allowed them to pass through to the Americans, who managed the transit camps in that area. Without further fanfare, the processing of the freed prisoners began, and Ray made his way home in several stages. He arrived home almost five years after he had left. His homecoming was sweet; in many ways the most important part was his reunion with Kathleen Burrows. They would be married very quickly thereafter. Ray also was finally ordained in the Presbyterian Church of Ireland. His future therefore seemed mapped out: he would serve as a clergyman, and always in partnership with Kathleen, for the rest of his life. But this young couple, although already accustomed to dramatic change, could not have foreseen the journey they would undertake in the years to come.

Ray and Kathleen knew that they needed some time to get their bearings, so Ray's assignment to a church in a Belfast suburb was a welcome respite. But soon the assignment came that would set their course for the future. Ray was appointed the first full-time Presbyterian chaplain at Queen's University. There was no job description for the young chaplain, so he and Kathleen had to figure it out for themselves. As they struggled to define his role, they drank seemingly endless cups of coffee and listened to students. The inspiration for the way forward came when Ray and Kathleen thought about his war years. He thought of his time at the YMCA Centre in Tobruk. It had been a meeting place for men under stress and in need. It had been a house of Christian foundation that was open to students of any faith or of none, where they could find encouragement and hope. If the idea had worked in Egypt, why not at the university?

The years that Ray and Kathleen Davey spent in student ministry at Queen's are a time of treasured memory for both the Daveys and the generation of students who were welcomed through the doors of the Presbyterian Centre at the university. Ever the good listeners, the Daveys became aware that the students of the 1950s and 1960s had new concerns. Whereas Ray's generation of students had been more content to debate the issues of the day, the students under the Daveys' ministry were more active and interested in applying their faith to concrete realities.

It was during this time that the idea which would make Corrymeela a reality began to emerge. It is important to remember that Corrymeela did not suddenly spring forth but was the result of a long and faithful journey taken together by the Daveys and the students. John Morrow was one of those students. Later he would succeed Ray as the leader of the Corrymeela Community. Morrow would later say that Ray Davey's greatest gift to the students was his ability to disclose their gifts to them and to help them integrate the new insights into their lives.[5]

A trip Ray took with the students to the Cottian Alps in 1952 made one of the deepest impressions on them. Their destination was the Agape Community, north of Turin. The founder of the Agape Community was Tullio Vinay, a pastor in the Waldensian Church. As a pastor in Florence during the war, Vinay had been responsible for saving many Jews. (For this heroic and costly act of grace, Tullio Vinay's name is inscribed in Jerusalem alongside the names of other "Righteous Gentiles.") After the war, Vinay took very seriously the struggle in Italian society between those who had collaborated with the Fascists and those who had been in the Resistance. Vinay challenged Italian students to do something practical to heal these social divisions. The result was the act of love — and great physical labor — that created Agape village. Because it was 5,000 feet above sea level, the work of bringing building materials up to the site was incredibly difficult. It took five summers for the students to complete their work, with students from thirty other nations joining the Italians. When the community was founded in 1950, Vinay said, "Feeling that we had been raised, as it were, from the dead by the mercy of God, we wanted to express our thankfulness to him who first loved us, by carving

5. Morrow, *Journey of Hope*, p. 97.

upon the rocks of our mountains His face, in its beautiful character of brotherly love."[6]

The Agape Community inspired its Irish visitors. They saw it as a place that shone a beacon of light — the kind of light they might also shine. Visiting the community was particularly moving for Ray, who had spent eighteen dreadful months as a prisoner of war in Italy. The community was created to be a place of openness where people could meet for work, prayer, and, above all, dialogue. Ray began to think about how the goals of this community might be applied in Northern Ireland. He thought of the social divisions of religion and class, of the complacency of much of church life, and of the way in which deep social and political problems were not discussed. Agape had given Ray, as well as his students, a vision of what might be.

The meaning of the visit to the Agape Community and how its concepts might be applied in Ireland were clarified for the Irish travelers on their way home. They stopped at Basel, Switzerland, where they stayed with like-minded friends. Ray asked his host if he had ever met Karl Barth, the world-famous Reformed theologian who lived in the city. Before long, a meeting had been arranged by his host, and Ray and his students went to see Barth, who received them warmly. Since Barth was receptive to students' questions, one of the visitors asked, "Sir, what can we do for world peace?" Barth replied, "Go home and set your own house in order."[7]

It is not the case that a visit to the Agape Community and a comment from Barth suddenly caused suggestible young Irishmen to forge into a life of community. Rather, these individuals undertook a journey of faith that led to the eventual success of Corrymeela. Looking back over the years, one can see turning points in the journey. There were other influences too, and important ones. The Iona Community and its powerfully attractive leader, George MacLeod, helped these Northern Irish Presbyterians learn that the church of God was meant to be a community,

6. Quoted by Morrow in *Journey of Hope*, p. 100.
7. Quoted in *A Channel of Peace*, p. 69.

not an aggregate of individuals. The Community of the Cross of Nails at Coventry Cathedral, where reconciliation was promoted by the indefatigable Horace Dammers, had a huge impact on the ideas that formed Corrymeela. In fact, one of the buildings at Corrymeela today is called Coventry House. From the French-Canadian lay Catholic leader Jean Vanier many Corrymeela people have learned the meaning of "embodied spirituality," Vanier's phrase for the acceptance of others. The influence of the French-American theologian-anthropologist René Girard was brought to Corrymeela by Dutch friends, especially Roel Kaptein, and caused community members to substantially rethink the meaning of the gospel message.[8]

The story of the Corrymeela Community would be a simple one if events had moved swiftly, but thirteen years stretched between the visit to Tullio Vinay and the Agape Community and the founding of Corrymeela in 1965. The deliberate pace was consistent with the democratic ideology established by Ray and Kathleen Davey at the Presbyterian Centre at Queen's. They believed in listening to all opinions, and they also believed that if a life in community would develop, it would do so at the right (God's own?) time. At one of the meetings with students to discuss the idea of community life, someone mentioned that the Holiday Fellowship Centre near Ballycastle was up for sale. Ray later commented that, from the first mention of the Ballycastle site, he thought it was just the right thing. Looking back now, Ray believes that their prayers — based, as he says, on a small and tentative faith — have been answered. When the purchase had been completed, a Corrymeela member, Janet Shepperson, put into words what many members felt:

I offer you this hope.
It is so small
The wind could blow it out.

8. These and other influences on the people of Corrymeela are discussed in detail by John Morrow in *Journey of Hope*.

Its feeble flickering
turns up in unexpected places
and seems to annoy those
with a big investment in dazzling light,
or in measuring the strength of darkness.
If this hope lives
it will be like swallows' wings,
erratic, unpredictable,
always on the move.
If this hope dies,
it will be buried shallow
like grass seed.[9]

During the summer of 1965, many members of Corrymeela and their friends worked on restoring the old house in Ballycastle. This group of amateur builders performed a miracle of grace in their work. When, on October 30, 1965, the Corrymeela Centre in Ballycastle was publicly dedicated, it was fitting that the words of dedication were spoken by Tullio Vinay, who traveled from the Agape Community for the occasion. His English may not have been perfect, but his thoughts were appropriate and challenging:

In this moment of deep emotion for me I wish that with the help of the Living Lord this centre may become:

FIRST: a place of preaching the New World as we see it in the person of Jesus Christ. The world needs to see this message in the real world of men. Here, living together, the New World in work and prayer, you may point it to all categories of men and push them to the same research, be they politicians, economists, sociologists, technicians, workers or students.

SECOND: a place of encounter and dialogue with all men, believers and unbelievers. The believers need the presence of the unbelievers, because they represent a criticism of our way of life; the unbelievers need us if we have real news to bring. A member

9. Quoted in *A Channel of Peace*, pp. 71-72.

of the Italian Parliament once said to me: "I am not religious but I am terribly attracted to Christ."

THIRD: to be a question-mark to the Church everywhere in Europe, so that they may review their structures and tasks, and be free from this instinct of preservation, to hear the time of God for its mission in the world.

FOURTH: more than all, that you — being together — have always open eyes and ears to understand when the Lord is passing nearby, to be ready to follow the way He shall indicate to you. As a Church we should not have an inferiority complex — not because we are or have something — but because every possibility is given to us as His instruments.[10]

Ray, as leader of the Corrymeela Community, responded by describing his vision for the work begun that day:

We hope that Corrymeela will come to be known as "the Open Village," open to all people of good will who are willing to meet each other, to learn from each other and work together for the good of all.

Open also for all sorts of new ventures and experiments in fellowship, study and worship.

Open to all sorts of people; from industry, the professions, agriculture and commerce.

This is part of our vision. We know we are only at the beginning and there is so much to be done.[11]

For Ray, his past and his future had become clear. He remembered his time as a prisoner in Italy and the harshness of it. Now from Italy had come a different voice and a different vision, "a vision of how the 'New World of Jesus Christ' might begin here in this place."[12]

10. Quoted in *A Channel of Peace*, pp. 76-77.
11. Quoted in *A Channel of Peace*, p. 77.
12. Quoted in *A Channel of Peace*, p. 77.

And so Corrymeela began in 1965 as an intentional community whose goal was to aid in seeking peace. It was not expressly founded to deal with "the troubles" of Northern Ireland. But, while the community never lost its dedication to seeking world-wide peace, the renewed violence of the winter of 1968-69 and afterward would provide a concrete reality in which to test that peaceful intentionality.

But it would be wrong to suggest that "the troubles" had a sudden impact on a community unaware of its social surroundings. Corrymeela members had long pursued ecumenical activities, and had long sought better understanding between Protestants and Catholics in Northern Ireland. Indeed, one of the first public conferences of the new community, held in April 1966, was called "Community 1966 — A Joint Protestant and Catholic Conference." The prime minister of Northern Ireland, Terence O'Neill, gave a memorable address. O'Neill was aware that it was nearly fifty years to the day that many Ulstermen had given their lives in the Battle of the Somme. It was also nearly fifty years to the day since the Easter Rising in Dublin. The prime minister's appeal was an apt conclusion for Corrymeela's first public conference:

> If we cannot be united in all things, let us be united in working to-
> gether in a Christian spirit to create better opportunities for our
> children, whether they be from the Falls Road or from Finaghy. In
> the enlightenment of education, in the dignity of work, in the se-
> curity of home and family, there are aims which all of us can pur-
> sue. As we advance to meet the promise of the future, let us shed
> the burdens of traditional grievances and ancient resentments.
> There is much we can do together. It must and — God willing —
> it will be done.[13]

The speech was much discussed in the press and elsewhere, thus giving Corrymeela more public recognition. *The Belfast Tele-*

13. Quoted in *A Channel of Peace*, p. 82.

graph said in its leading article, "Through Captain O'Neill and those who organized the community conference, Corrymeela takes its place in Irish history."[14]

It would take an entire book to explore the life of Corrymeela, which has been in existence now for more than three decades. The struggles and triumphs of the community as it has striven to assist in the changing of attitudes and lives is a story of complexity and of integrity: complexity because of the diversity of experiences; integrity because of the fidelity to certain beliefs. Although Corrymeela has had an impact on people in Northern Ireland and beyond in diverse ways, the community has held fast to certain principles. They are engagingly put in the form of a question by the historian of Corrymeela, Alf McCreary: "Can the Christian message break through the structures — political, social and ecclesiastical — that imprison society in general, and in so doing bring liberation and hope for every man and woman?"[15]

This story — of unmasking evil structures and of liberating people — can perhaps be best illustrated through the lives of some ordinary people. They were caught up in "the troubles," and they found refuge, acceptance, peace, and reconciliation at Corrymeela. Let us listen to some of their stories.

In 1971 the political situation had deteriorated to its lowest ebb. Violence was everywhere, and seemingly beyond the control of the law and security forces. The government made a final desperate attempt to restore order by initiating internment without trial. This only served to provoke violence on both sides. In some urban areas, people who were living on the margins of tribal turf or in enclaves within the territory of "the other side" were intimidated, beaten or otherwise wounded, and turned out of their homes; some were killed. This burden fell on both sides of the divide, but disproportionately on the Catholic/Nationalist side as Protestant/Unionist terrorists tried to burn them out. A Corrymeela member was living and working in a run-down Catholic/Na-

---

14. Quoted in *A Channel of Peace*, p. 82.
15. *Corrymeela: Hill of Harmony in Northern Ireland*, p. 112.

71

tionalist area of West Belfast. She appealed to Ray Davey at the Ballycastle Centre of Corrymeela to provide refuge for the families at risk. Ray agreed at once. The facilities were soon overrun, so Ray appealed to schools in the community for temporary shelter and asked local businesses for food and clothing for the Belfast refugees. He later commented, "Now the town knew what Corrymeela was about and that we meant what we said."[16]

Listen to the story told by one of the mothers, Margaret Mulvenna:

> On the morning of Internment, 9th August 1971, we were awakened out of our beds by squealing and yelling and the sound of army Saracens [armored personnel carriers] driving round the streets. Men and boys were dragged from their beds and taken away. It was an awful experience to come through and it made me feel very bitter towards the soldiers and I knew my eldest daughter and two eldest sons felt exactly the same way. Only for the Grace of God and my maternal instinct to protect my family at all cost, we too could be a part of the violence which exists in Northern Ireland today. For two days and nights we lay on the floor in our sitting room, we could not go to bed, as the IRA and the British soldiers were in a non-stop gun fight.
>
> On the third morning, at about 6:30 a.m., the shooting stopped. I went to the front door and saw the soldiers had surrounded the estate, and the shooting was over for a while. We gathered what clothes and food we could and we walked out of that estate. No one was allowed to go in or out. I shall never forget the commanding officer's face as I got to the road block with my seven children all clutching each other's hands. He just looked at us and the tears ran down his face as he commanded his men to let us through.
>
> We made our way to a school about half a mile away and I was told there was a bus leaving Belfast. We all got into the bus. I did not know where it was going but I was so glad to get away I didn't

16. Quoted in *A Channel of Peace*, p. 85.

care. This I would say, thank God, was the turning point of my life, this journey was to lead me to a people I didn't know existed, a people who cared and until the day I die I shall never be able to thank those people enough. The bus arrived at a little seaside town on the very north of Ireland. It was called Ballycastle and as I was stepping out of the bus a tall gentle-looking man took my hand to help me. His words will always be implanted in my mind; they were: "You will be all right now." I do not think he even knew the comfort and strength I got from those six words. For four years I had been on my own in the world, but since that meeting I have never been alone.

I will never forget the kindness we received in those difficult days, the meals that were provided for us in the school canteen, the sleeping quarters in the gym and how the students looked after the children, organizing games and taking them down to the shore and sand. That first stay in Ballycastle was a turning point in our lives. I believe, although I am a devout Catholic, it was my first real experience of Christianity. From then on I began to live and think reconciliation. I became a member of the Community four years later. Corrymeela involvement is the one thing in my life I shall always be grateful for. Many times my children and I could have been caught up in the turmoil and bitterness brought on by years of unrest, such as tragic deaths, Army harassment and the Hunger Strike. But thanks be to God with the help of the Corrymeela Community and the prayers and support of other members, we have remained true to our commitment to work for peace and justice till this day.[17]

Such experiences had a dramatic effect on the core members of the Corrymeela Community, most of whom were Protestants in those early years. Most of the people helped by Corrymeela were Catholics because, in the community's early years, they were the group most at risk. The profound result, in both the community and the surrounding region, was a clear realization that there would be no

17. Quoted in *A Channel of Peace*, pp. 86-87.

turning back on the way of peace, and that this sort of peace-seeking would be costly.

There is also the story of Peg Healy, whose son Desmond had been mistakenly killed by the police. The teenager was coming back from a shop with a bottle of sauce. When the police spotted him, they mistook the bottle for a gasoline bomb and assumed that Desmond was ready to throw it at them. They did warn him, but when the boy did not respond, they killed him. Peg Healy explains how the news devastated her family — and how Corrymeela helped:

I just did not dare to believe that Desmond was dead. I could not accept it at first. Then when I began to realize what had happened a terrible hatred welled up in me. My son Michael went wild. He wanted to kill all around him. I had an awful job preventing him from joining some organization. All he wanted was revenge. Give Michael a gun and he would have murdered everybody.

I could not even pass soldiers in the street without shouting at them. When I heard the news that soldiers had been killed I did not care how many were lying dead. I thought "maybe that's the one that shot my child," I didn't even care about their mothers. It was their fault for letting them come to Ireland. I just looked at the soldiers as animals. God, how I hated them.

About a year after the boy's death the Legion of Mary sent us to Corrymeela. I think Corrymeela was the first thing that brought Ted [Desmond's twin] to realize that he had to live, because before that he wouldn't have gone anywhere. He just didn't seem to want to mix with anybody at all. It was the best thing that ever happened, because it took him out of himself. He met people from all parts of the world. He made friends even, and he is good with children. And Corrymeela helped him to find a steady job. Corrymeela is so homely. The housekeeper, Anna Glass, is very nice and she was good to us. And others too.

Going to Corrymeela helped my younger son, Michael. He really showed his brother's death. He was ready to knife the soldiers, throw stones and everything else. I didn't know what was going to happen to him. I was afraid to let him through the front door. He had this thing about Protestants, they were as bad as the army. He would not trust anybody but Catholics. But Corrymeela did help him. There he realized that all Protestants were not bad and all Catholics were not good. Corrymeela made a terrific difference to him. I think it also helped me. I still go to Mass but I have not taken the Sacraments, except once, since the boy died. A priest in the chapel said, "If you can't forgive your enemy there is no point in taking Communion." Well, I couldn't forgive. One priest I really liked said, "God does not expect you to forgive suddenly. It will come." He asked me if I wanted to take Communion and I did, the next morning. . . .

One day at Corrymeela I remember coming back to my room and I found the bedclothes in tatters and my own clothes all torn. Somebody had written "Fenian bastards." I was ready to go home. I felt everyone was against me. The leaders were terribly upset. They turned over everything to find out who had done it and they talked me into staying.

About four days later I was told who did it. It was a wee boy whose father and mother had abandoned him, and he was with a bunch of orphans at Corrymeela. I realized that he was not bad, only jealous of Michael and Danny because they had a mother. He really was looking for a bit of love. After that he came to me every night, and I took him on my knee. Maybe I learnt something from that.

It was Ray Davey, the leader of the Corrymeela Community, who made the difference about the soldiers. It was just the way he talked and listened. I'm still not too much in love with soldiers, but I suppose you have to stop hating. I began to think of the soldiers' mothers, or their wives or children; a life is a life. Maybe some of them have been through what I've been through.

It is only lately that I stop myself from shouting at them in the street. I still don't like them, but now I turn my back to them. I don't know about this thing forgiveness. But I do know that Corrymeela helped me and it helped Michael and Danny and Ted.

I don't know how it will go in the end, but I suppose we'll have to live together no matter what way it goes.[18]

The refugees, by the hundreds, came to a place of welcome where questions were not asked. For many of the guests, a real distinction began to emerge between religion (which for them meant sectarian bigotry) and Christianity (which meant acceptance, love, and care). One little girl confided to a Corrymeela member, "My mummy knows what is wrong with this country. It's them Protestants." The member said that she herself was a Protestant. The girl responded, "But ah, you are not a Protestant when you are at Corrymeela."[19] When this kind of unconditional love is given and received, words are often intrusions and the labels "Protestant" and "Catholic" irrelevant.

The case of one boy is similarly instructive. His father had been killed by the police, and his brother had been murdered by IRA terrorists. He was brought, inconsolable, to Corrymeela. After many days, Ray Davey asked the boy if anything might be done for him. He asked to be taken to his brother's grave. The next day Ray drove him to Belfast and found the grave, and the two spent a long time together there. Later on, back at Corrymeela, the boy's grief began to subside; it was as if he could begin to accept his brother's death only after he saw the grave. This simple act of grace — although it took an entire day from the schedule of a busy man — was a great help to the recovery of this broken boy. It was done mostly without words, but the message of acceptance and love was clear.[20]

These early experiences taught the Corrymeela Community some important lessons: that the work of the community would be difficult and unpredictable, and thus they would have to be flexible; and that the community could do that work fully and well if it was not defined, by precept and example, as a Protestant community. This proved difficult at first, since some of the members were

18. Quoted in *A Channel of Peace*, pp. 90-92.
19. Quoted in *Corrymeela: Hill of Harmony in Northern Ireland*, p. 68.
20. *Corrymeela: Hill of Harmony in Northern Ireland*, p. 69.

intent on having a theological basis for the community's work. It is not that these people were rigid or conservative (peacemakers in community are neither of these things) but that they wanted to state their intentions clearly. In the end it was decided that the basis for membership would be simply this: "We believe in God as revealed in Jesus Christ and in the continuing work of the Holy Spirit." Theology, as such, would be developed as the community dealt with specific problems and situations.

In this context, one might have expected the Corrymeela Community to have developed a lowest-common-denominator type of ecumenical theology, and definitely more applied than abstract. However, while an accessible theology of incarnational acceptance did develop, the Corrymeela Community would learn much from the work of anthropologist-theologian René Girard, a thinker not known widely beyond high-level academic circles and surely not known for accessibility. Girard, for many years a professor at Stanford University, wrote several important books in developing his unique view of religion in general and of Christianity in particular. His best-known works are *Violence and the Sacred* (1977) and *The Scapegoat* (1986). His work was distilled and brought to the Corrymeela Community by Roel Kaptein, a Dutch theologian and psychotherapist.

As early as 1974, the people of the Netherlands had established a committee of concern about Northern Ireland in their own Dutch Reformed Church. But it was from 1980 on that the connection between Corrymeela and their Dutch comrades really began to grow and deepen. It was Roel Kaptein, who introduced the thinking of René Girard to the community, who forged the closest relationship with them. John Morrow provides a good summary of the Girard-Kaptein influence on Corrymeela in his book *Journey of Hope.*[21]

There are two concepts in Girard's systematic theology that

21. The following is drawn from *Journey of Hope*, pp. 68-77, and from Leo D. Lefebure, "Victims, Violence and the Sacred: The Thought of René Girard," *Christian Century*, 11 December 1996, pp. 1226-29.

must be underscored: mimesis and scapegoating. In his examination of mimesis, Girard describes the essence of human conflict; in his discussion of scapegoating, he demonstrates the ways in which societies (often with religion's help) have used scapegoating as a way to deal with violence and evil. For Girard (and for Kaptein, who explicated these ideas at Corrymeela), the antidote is to be found in Christianity, and above all in the crucifixion and resurrection of Jesus. A brief review of Girard's ideas will prove helpful here.

Girard believed that all human relationships are in "mimesis" — that is, all of us are living in unconscious imitation of someone else's thoughts and desires. As human cultures develop, this desire for similar things leads to conflict. Further, because this "mimesis of desire" escalates to socially uncontrollable levels and leads to violence, a way of stabilizing societies has involved projecting the difficulties on one member or one group (scapegoating) and directing the violence at them. From his theological viewpoint, Girard interprets the story of the Israelites in an astonishingly different way. As he sees it, God identifies with the victims who have been cast out of Egypt. The story of Jesus brings to a climax the lie of scapegoating. The scapegoat is now, in a way, God himself. Humans — all of us — must accept our common sinfulness. In the reality of God's act of grace, we can no longer project evil on others, but must accept that we are all evil, and that we might all be good one day.

Whether or not Girard's theology is normatively correct is not at issue here. The point is that for many of the leaders of the Corrymeela Community, Girard's insights, as explained by Roel Kaptein, enabled them to read the gospel in a new way. For John Morrow, they were a fresh way of saying what Presbyterians have always heard, that "all have sinned and fallen short of the glory of God." These insights also renewed the community's ideas about human solidarity that cross the conventional lines of "us and them." In the end, if Girard is right that "the mimesis of desire" explains relationships, then those desiring Christ together have broken through into a new community that dissolves artificial boundaries. In the context of Northern Ireland and its "history of troubles," this could be a powerful witness for peace, renewal, and reconciliation.

While the impact of Girard on Corrymeela is undeniable, it would be a mistake to suggest that Corrymeela has become a theological debating society. On the contrary, the vast majority of Corrymeela members are engaged in the practical, day-to-day work of acceptance and listening. John Morrow's son, Duncan — himself a well-known academic scholar and admirer of Girard — says that the work of Corrymeela has been and still is with ordinary people in Northern Ireland and beyond. While not diminishing the impact of Girard and of the community's good friend Kaptein, he points out that the ministry and witness of Corrymeela has been, and remains, the work of bringing former enemies together in an atmosphere that does not ask questions about the past, and of bringing people who have suffered much to a place of harmony.[22]

I began this discussion of Corrymeela with an evocation of its place along the Antrim coastline. In conclusion I will return us there. It was June 2, 1998, and the occasion was the dedication of the New House, a complete rebuilding of the white house that, for a generation of visitors, had symbolized Corrymeela. The New House was a new beginning for Corrymeela, all the more fitting because this year marked a new beginning in Northern Irish politics. The New House and The Agreement are good examples of the way forward. That day in June, when the sun came out and His Royal Highness Prince Charles joined political and religious leaders in the celebration, evoked another day, nearly thirty-three years earlier, when a group of young people joined Ray Davey in affirming the reconciling power of God.

Ray Davey spoke again, his hair a bit whiter now but his resolve still strong. His vision for the future was that, as always, Corrymeela stand for transforming a culture of violence into a cul-

22. Author's conversation with Dr. Duncan Morrow, Department of Politics, University of Ulster, 20 September 1997.

ture of peace. But, taking note of the new Agreement, he added that the task before all of us now was to create a culture of forgiveness. He summed up the longings and prayers of Corrymeela's history, and the desires of all those there on that festive day, in the words of the poet Seamus Heaney:

> History says don't hope
> On this side of the grave.
> But then, once in a lifetime
> The longed-for tidal wave
> Of justice can rise up,
> And hope and history rhyme.
> So hope for a great sea-change
> On the far side of revenge.
> Believe that a further shore
> Is reachable from here.[23]

23. The remarks of Ray Davey and the lines quoted from Heaney are from *Corrymeela News: The Journal of the Corrymeela Community*, Summer 1998, p. 5.

The Christian Renewal Centre

The Christian Renewal Centre (CRC) is located almost as far to the south in Northern Ireland as Corrymeela is to the north. The CRC can be found just outside the town of Rostrevor in County Down, about fifty miles south of Belfast. It is about half-way between the border town of Newry and the fishing village of Kilkeel. The nineteenth-century Irish song that celebrates a place "where the mountains of Mourne sweep down to the sea" could have been written about the Centre. Indeed, the Mourne mountains are directly behind the main building of the CRC, and the Irish Sea is about a hundred yards from its front door. The sea is tranquil at that spot because it forms an inlet known as Carlingford Lough.

What is now the Christian Renewal Centre was built in Victorian times as a holiday retreat for a member of the establishment, the Earl of Kilmorey. But the Centre, which has become home to a Christian community, was founded for more serious purposes than holidays. Of course, both the community members and the guests enjoy the beautiful setting, but it reminds every visitor why the Centre is there. Standing in the front garden, one often sees a gunboat about halfway across the lough, where a national boundary line exists between the United Kingdom and the Republic of Ireland. Moreover, in the town center of Rostrevor and the neighboring town, Warrenpoint, the eye soon sees the physical signs of the

81

strife and violence that have torn Northern Ireland apart for a generation.

The person who had the idea for the Centre, and who has been the moving force behind its work, is Cecil Kerr. He is a man of gentle spirit with sparkling, captivating eyes, a ready wit, and, above all, deep insight into the spiritual dimensions of "the troubles." Like Ray Davey at Corrymeela, Cecil Kerr would want our attention to be focused elsewhere, first on the Holy Spirit and then on the many people who have supported the work of the Christian Renewal Centre since its founding a quarter-century ago. He would point thankfully to Walter Skelsey, Patricia Moore, Stephanie Crowther, Fanny Robertson, David Gillett, Eric and Mabel Mayer, Niall Griffin, and Harry Smith, as well as hundreds of others, not the least of which is his wife, Myrtle.

Cecil Kerr was born and raised in Enniskillen, county Fermanagh, in the southwestern part of what is now Northern Ireland. While the town was made up of equal proportions of Protestants and Catholics, the two communities lived apart as much as possible. Cecil, growing up in Enniskillen during World War II, had only one Catholic friend. Here was a young man whose British family had been in Ireland for about three centuries. That he had virtually no encounters with the native Irish says a great deal about the divided society in which he grew up.[1]

Cecil was raised in a conventional home and was associated with the (Anglican) Church of Ireland, as much for cultural as for religious reasons. But when he was a teenager, he experienced a powerful conversion that put him on the road to (what they call in evangelical circles) "full-time Christian work." After completing his secondary education at Portora Royal School, he enrolled in Trinity College, Dublin, to study Hebrew and Oriental languages. One would think that since he was attending the most prestigious

1. These comments about Cecil Kerr's life and work are taken from interviews with the author conducted on 15 January 1991 and 6 October 1998 in Rostrevor, and from his book *The Way of Peace* (London: Hodder & Stoughton, 1990). Subsequent references to this work will be made parenthetically in the text.

university in Ireland, located in a city in which nine out of ten people are Catholics, this young Ulsterman would have broadened his
experience. But in fact, in the 1950s, Trinity was still the
Protestant university in Ireland, partly because the Catholic
Church discouraged its brightest young people from going to a pre-
dominantly Protestant institution.

Cecil's meeting of Myrtle, the woman who would become his
wife, brought him both love and "a considerable challenge to my
narrow northern upbringing" (*WP*, p. 27). Paradoxically, it was this
woman, an evangelical from the Republic of Ireland, who began to
broaden Cecil's horizons, a process that would culminate in this
young man's becoming one of the leading Protestant activists in
Irish reconciliation. He says of Myrtle,

> I had never before met a Protestant who spoke Irish. Myrtle was
> brought up in a Church of Ireland family near Mullingar in the
> Irish Midlands. In a largely Roman Catholic area she had experi-
> enced much closer and neighborly contacts than I had. My inher-
> ited Unionism was something of a shock to her and her under-
> standing of Irish nationalism was an even greater shock to me.
> (*WP*, p. 23)

It is with this combination of deep love and mixed political orien-
tations that Cecil and Myrtle began their life together in Northern
Ireland. Having been ordained, Cecil had his first clerical appointment at St. Patrick's, a Church of Ireland parish in Coleraine.

The significant change came in the young Reverend Kerr's life
in 1965, when he was appointed the Church of Ireland chaplain at
Queen's University, and pastor of the Church of Ireland church on
campus, the Church of the Resurrection. For the first time in his
working life, the young chaplain was thrust into a dynamic, multi-
cultural community of learning. About half the five thousand students at Queen's were Catholic, the other half Protestant. For the
first time, Kerr had ecumenical colleagues, including the Catholic
Father Tony Farquahar, the Methodist David Tuttle, and the Presbyterian Ray Davey, the most influential of the three. Ray Davey

was the "senior" chaplain in every sense of the word, and the younger chaplains — especially Cecil Kerr — readily acknowledge their debt to him. Kerr offers this recollection:

> Ray Davey's vision of reconciliation was a constant challenge and inspiration to us. While working with the YMCA during the Second World War he was taken prisoner in North Africa. His experiences of sharing with Christians of other denominations in a prisoner of war camp taught him many important lessons about unity in Christ across the traditional barriers. In such a crucible of suffering ancient prejudices were melted. In many ways Ray foresaw the gathering storm in Ulster and in positive ways he and others who shared his vision prepared for it. Under his leadership the community of reconciliation which is now Corrymeela was born. I was privileged to be closely involved with him in some of the early projects in setting up that house of peace on the north Antrim coast. We used to take work parties of students to Corrymeela. Facing the challenge of working together to restore an old building forged lasting friendships across many inherited barriers. Ray and I presided over fervent discussions with the students late into the night. During such times, possibilities opened to us of finding new ways of living together in our divided land. (*WP*, p. 24)

The 1960s were a time of great turmoil in academic institutions, and Queen's was no exception. But the new freedom for discussion and inquiry that all students felt became particularly focused; in the Ulster context, the focus was on the political and social questions that were coming to a head. Cecil Kerr and Ray Davey believed that if Christianity was to be a vital force in Northern Ireland, it had to speak to the issues being forced into public attention, first by the legitimate protest of Queen's students and the Northern Ireland Civil Rights Association, and later by the terrorism of the Provisional wing of the IRA. As Kerr himself has admitted, he felt powerless in the developing circumstances. He faced something of a crisis in his calling. On one level, his ministry at Queen's was very successful. He was good with students, and with the help of his partner in the gospel, Myrtle, their home and the Church of the Resurrection were centers of good and much-appreciated activity. But Cecil was deeply concerned about certain questions: Couldn't Christianity speak more positively to the desperate circumstances in West Belfast? Was there no power that could change this seemingly endless sectarian strife?

In the late 1960s, Kerr did not realize that his calling would be to begin a new community dedicated to Christian reconciliation. As much as he appreciated the efforts of Ray Davey and the Corrymeela people, he did not see himself emulating his former colleague by founding another residential community. In Davey's case, the call to Christian community was a long process, with discernible steps along the way. For Kerr, the call would come suddenly and unexpectedly, and it would change his life. He would experience a direct calling from God, or, as he would put it, an outpouring of the Holy Spirit.

In the spring of 1971, when Ulster was in deep turmoil because of violence and when Kerr was honestly casting about for his future direction, he happened to meet three Americans on the Queen's campus. They were from the Church of the Redeemer in Houston, Texas, a parish of the American Episcopal Church that had experienced a dramatic renewal. At first, Kerr did not know what to make of these visitors. "Their accounts of the miracles wrought through the Holy Spirit seemed to conservative ears rather unlikely, if not bizarre," he recalls (*WP*, p. 26). When asked why they had come to Belfast, the visitors replied, "The Holy Spirit sent us" (*WP*, p. 27). They further explained that they had no prior knowledge of Belfast other than what they called "a word of prophecy" they had received in a meeting in Houston which told them to go. Kerr ultimately was to warm to these strange Americans because their testimonies about the word of God among them rang true. Later on, after he himself visited the church in Houston and had a good conversation with its rector, Graham Pulkingham, Kerr had a new vision of what might happen in Ireland if the whole church would be open to the Spirit. At that time Kerr read the J. B. Phillips version of Acts, and it showed him again what was possible with God:

> Here we are seeing the Church in its first youth, valiant and un-spoiled — a body of ordinary men and women joined in an uncon-querable fellowship never before seen on this earth. Yet we can-not help feeling disturbed as well as moved, for this surely is the Church as it was meant to be. It is vigorous and flexible, for these are the days before it ever became fat and short of breath through prosperity, or muscle-bound by over-organisation. These men did not make "acts of faith," they believed; they did not "say their prayers," they really prayed. They did not hold conferences on psychosomatic medicine, they simply healed the sick. But if they were uncomplicated and naïve by modern standards we have rue-fully to admit that they were open on the God-ward side in a way that is almost unknown today. No one can read this book without being convinced that there is Someone here at work besides mere human beings. Perhaps because of their very simplicity, perhaps because of their readiness to believe, to obey, to give, to suffer, and if need be to die, the Spirit of God found what surely he must always be seeking — a fellowship of men and women so united in love and faith that he can work in them and through them with the minimum of let or hindrance. Consequently it is a matter of sober historical fact that never before has any small body of ordinary people so moved the world that their enemies could say, with tears of rage in their eyes, that these men "have turned the world upside down!" (*WP,* p. 30)

In 1972 Kerr began a systematic inquiry into the whole notion of "baptism in the Holy Spirit." He wanted for his life and minis-try the power promised to the New Testament church. But he did not want to rush after what some people thought of as a passing phase in the church. Cecil and Myrtle decided to go on a retreat with some Queen's students and with Roy Millar, a Belfast sur-geon, and his wife, Rosemary. During that weekend, the Millars were to lead a Bible study and share their experiences of baptism in the Holy Spirit. On one occasion, other retreat participants prayed for Cecil with the laying on of hands. At the time, nothing discernible happened. But later on, while praying in his own room, he reports being "aware of the presence of God, like a loving Father offering me all the inheritance he had promised, and asking me to receive it as a gift" (*WP*, p. 34).

Now to many readers this might not seem like an earth-shattering occasion because it was unaccompanied by extraordinary experience. Just so, says Kerr. In reply to an oft-asked question — "Surely you had the Holy Spirit in your life prior to this, as a Christian and a minister?" — Kerr replies, "Yes, I had the Holy Spirit living in me as he does in every believer. But now the Holy Spirit had me in a way that was not so before" (*WP*, p. 34). After her own initial doubts and questions were answered, Myrtle joined her husband in a baptism of the Holy Spirit. Together the partners went forward with a renewed sense of purpose.

Northern Ireland has had many dark years since 1969. Perhaps 1973 was one of the worst. The good folk of Ulster who lived through those days, and those of us who visited friends and colleagues there, would agree that it was a dark time indeed. David Gillett, a young English cleric, later wrote about those years, and the title of his book describes them well: *The Darkness Where God Is.*[2] Many Christians felt powerless in the depths of the darkness. They had prayed about "the troubles" for many years, and to no apparent avail. Many non-Christians noted the religious roots of the conflict, and they either mocked Christians for still believing or gave up on the gospel altogether. For the latter group, it seemed like nonsense to say, "Religion has failed; give us more religion." Christians, for their part, agreed, or should have done so. Indeed, many Christians should have said something more like "Religion has failed; give us Christianity."

In truth, the Christian religion in Ireland had become compartmentalized in denominational boxes, divided by the social realities of ethnicity and social class. Working-class Protestants on Shankhill

---

2. David Gillett, *The Darkness Where God Is: Reconciliation and Renewal in Northern Ireland* (Eastbourne, U.K.: Kingsway Publications, 1983).

Road who worshipped at a gospel hall rarely met the middle-class Church of Ireland members in Holywood, or the equally middle-class Presbyterians along Malone Road. And very few of the Protestants of any social class had much to do with either urban or rural Catholics. Many Christians agreed with Cecil Kerr (as they did with Ray Davey) that there would be little progress toward a political solution in Ireland unless and until there was some progress in overcoming enmity and divisiveness among Christian groups.

During 1973 Kerr had several new experiences that underscored the continuing parallel of darkness and light. The occasion that was simultaneously the most exciting and the most unnerving for him was the time he was invited to come back to his hometown of Enniskillen to lead a youth outreach program, an annual event that required school presentations and open-air meetings. The invitation committee was composed of the three main Protestant churches — Presbyterian, Methodist, and Church of Ireland. Kerr accepted the invitation on the condition that he be allowed to bring along a group of Christian students from Belfast and Dublin, both Protestant and Roman Catholic. Still, he felt uneasy about this new course of ministry. He would be taking his new vision of Christians together back to his hometown, where the "normal" pattern of religious division was the rule. He knew what Protestant hardliners would say about a local man, who knew the rules of society, who came back to Enniskillen with a "mixed" group of students.

During the time the team spent in Enniskillen, there was a short outdoor service that was led by a Catholic priest and several nuns. Kerr remembers the experience vividly, and its cost:

> As I stood there I suddenly began to feel a great fear coming over me. I sensed that as the cars drove past many of my friends and relatives were looking at me. In my mind . . . I could see them rolling down the windows of their cars and shouting "You are a traitor." Then I had an almost physical sensation of a bullet being shot into my back. It was all so frighteningly real to me that I had to ask my brothers and sisters from both traditions to pray that I would be delivered from that fear. (*WP*, p. 45)

Nevertheless, the group persisted, and prayed that those opposing the student team would be released from the prison houses of the heart and mind, where they were so sure they had God in their own boxes.

Kerr had another significant experience in 1973: the vision for the Christian Renewal Centre began to come clear to him. The CRC would be a place where Christians of all denominations could come to pray and work together for an Ireland united in Christ. Kerr believed that a community of men and women should live together to model this new way of worship, work, and service. Further, both he and his wife had the deep conviction that, just as they had learned from each other about "north and south," the CRC should be near the border in order to facilitate the meeting of Irish folk both from the United Kingdom province of Ulster and from the rest of the Republic of Ireland. The area outside the town of Rostrevor seemed ideal.

Kerr was ordained in the Church of Ireland, which meant he was under the pastoral care and direction of his bishop. Being an Anglican, Kerr could not just go off, in free-enterprise style, and found a reconciliation community on his own. Kerr's ordination had implications for the work he hoped to begin at Rostrevor. So early in 1975 he met with his bishop, Dr. Arthur Butler, to discuss his idea. The bishop's first concern was for Myrtle and the children, and his second concern for the ministry of pastoral care at Queen's. But as the two spoke further about Kerr's vision, the importance of it became clear to the bishop, who said these welcome words: "I believe God is calling you to do this new work and I believe the place is right and the time is ripe" (*WP*, p. 54). Kerr also knew enough to consult with George Quinn, the bishop of Restrover's diocese. Quinn's support would be important if the Centre was to take shape in Rostrevor. As it turned out, he was very willing to give that support. So, in Kerr's mind, all was confirmed: he believed himself called by God to do this new work; friends in Belfast and the students at Queen's were encouraging; and the two relevant bishops of the Church of Ireland were supportive.

Just as all these things were coming together, another bishop — not knowing of the Rostrevor plan — asked Kerr about his interest in a large and important parish. What should he do now? Kerr asked Dr. Butler's opinion, and the bishop's response was convincing: "God has clearly called you to this work and given you the vision for it. Someone else will be able to undertake the work of the parish, but if you do not do the work you feel called to it may never be done and the opportunity may not come again" (*WP*, p. 57). Things moved quite quickly after that. The property at Rostrevor was purchased after a final financial problem was overcome, and friends went ahead to prepare it. The Kerrs moved down to Rostrevor from Belfast on August 22, 1974.

The community of like-minded people that Cecil and Myrtle Kerr gathered around them in Rostrevor was intentionally focused on Christian unity and reconciliation. As Cecil explains, "Our unity as brothers and sisters in Christ would have to demonstrate in practical ways the unity Christ desires for his people. That meant providing a place of welcome for all who came; an open house where people could find the Lord in each other" (*WP*, p. 66).

The community at Rostrevor has often been amused by the way weekend visitors think it a sort of heaven-on-earth to live in a lovely setting, in constant prayer and in fellowship. Happily for the Centre, one of its earliest members helped other members with their initial thinking along these lines. Walter Skelsey, who had a great deal of experience with the Scargill Community in Yorkshire, England, led other members of Rostrevor through Dietrich Bonhoeffer's writings about community. This kind of Christian realism was of great importance as the CRC began its mission. Kerr explains:

> Innumerable times a whole Christian community has broken down because it had sprung from a wish dream. The serious Christian, set down for the first time in a Christian community, is likely to bring with him a very definite idea of what Christian life together should be and try to realise it. But God's grace speedily shatters such dreams. Just as surely God desires to lead us to a

knowledge of genuine Christian fellowship, so surely must we be overwhelmed by a great general disillusionment with others, with Christians in general, and, if we are fortunate, with ourselves. By sheer grace God will not permit us to live even for a brief period in a dream world. He does not abandon us to those rapturous experiences and lofty moods that come over us like a dream. God is not a God of the emotions but the God of truth. Only that fellowship which faces such disillusionment, with all its unhappy and ugly aspects, begins to be what it should be in God's sight, begins to grasp in faith the promise that is given to it. The sooner this shock of disillusionment comes to an individual and to a community the better for both. A community which cannot bear and cannot survive such a crisis, which insists upon keeping its illusion when it should be shattered, permanently loses in that moment the promise of Christian community. Sooner or later it will collapse. Every human wish dream that is injected into the Christian community is a hindrance to genuine community and must be banished if genuine community is to survive. (*WP*, pp. 66-67)

A further resource for the Christian Renewal Centre as it sought to develop an effective community of love and reconciliation was encouragement from leaders and lay people from other faith traditions. I have already mentioned Cahal Daly several times in this book. That Catholic prelate has been a source of enormous support for all peace-seeking Protestants. The community in Rostrevor found particularly welcome the cardinal's comments at a British church-leaders' conference on Northern Ireland:

The Church cannot identify itself with any political community. A Christian preacher speaks to the whole people of God, and not to members of the unionist party or the nationalist party. The Gospel is for all men, and not just for a politically homogeneous group. The Kingdom of God is a universal kingdom, not a political faction. When Churchmen say "our people," they must not confine the phrase to people of one political persuasion. Indeed, I am convinced that our ministry of reconciliation summons all of us churchmen in our political situation in Northern Ireland to try to speak across the denominational divides and to address ourselves to both communities. We must never assert the rights of one community without also affirming the rights of the other community. In matters where the faith touches on political and social responsibilities, we must not speak out of or to "our own people" only; we must try to speak for and to the other community as well. To work to reconcile the two communities is our bounden duty as servants of God's universal Kingdom of justice, forgiveness, brotherhood, love, and peace.

There are many churchmen in Northern Ireland who in this time of turmoil and tension have spoken this prophetic word and have been listened to with respect by many in their own community and beyond it. They deserve the admiration and gratitude of all for their courage and integrity. They deserve the support of all for their Christian leadership. One does not exaggerate in comparing their witness to that of the Confessing Church in Hitler's Germany. (*WP,* p. 152)

With these sources of caution, inspiration, and support, the Christian Renewal Centre began, and over the years it has sustained a highly successful ministry of reconciliation and peace. A realist, however, might want to ask the visionaries at Rostrevor and elsewhere this question: Can people really change, and is religion the key to that change? Well, the reply comes, to the realist let us say this: No military solution to the Northern Ireland conflict could be found. In any case, now that The Agreement has provided a framework for peace, the main question in Northern Ireland has moved to the matter of reconciliation: Now that peace has come, can the former enemies be civil to each other, even friendly? Can the bitter enmities be broken down, and can there be forgiveness for past hurts? In this specific regard, Cecil Kerr values highly the words of Martin Luther King, who a few years before his death wrote, "He who is devoid of the power to forgive is devoid of the power to love. Forgiveness is a catalyst creating the atmosphere necessary for a fresh start and a new beginning" (*WP,* p. 186).

The question of whether people can really change in response to the gospel is difficult to answer definitively. But, for supporters of the Christian Renewal Centre and other activists in reconciliation efforts in Northern Ireland, the testimonies of ordinary people are a significant witness to their belief. As Cecil Kerr often says, "rays of hope are piercing the darkness" in Northern Ireland. Let us look at some examples.

David Hamilton was a Loyalist prisoner in the Crumlin Road prison in Belfast, serving a sentence for armed robbery as a member of a terrorist organization. One day, when a team from the Renewal Centre was giving presentations and leading worship in the prison, Cecil Kerr sensed that he had "a word of knowledge" from God to share. Even though the surroundings made this all a bit strange, Kerr reluctantly said what he felt: "I believe that God is speaking to at least one man here who is going to become an evangelist, who will win many people to Christ" (*WP*, p. 163). Hamilton later wrote Kerr that someone else had expressed a similar view about him. Kerr's suggestion from God had confirmed the direction that Hamilton was already considering. When Hamilton was released from prison, his evangelical zeal and his ex-prisoner status made him a logical choice to work with the Irish branch of Prison Fellowship (an international organization founded by Chuck Colson in America). For several years thereafter, he worked with and ministered to prisoners and their families. And he worked with more than just Loyalist prisoners. He befriended an ex-Republican terrorist, Liam McCloskey, one of the hunger strikers of 1981 who did not die. McCloskey has since renounced violence and become a committed Christian. It is a remarkable witness for peace and reconciliation when two formerly sworn enemies — David Hamilton, a Protestant, and Liam McCloskey, a Catholic — share a platform together to give witness to the transforming possibilities of God's love in people's lives.

And then there are the stories of people who have been touched by the violence but yet have had the grace to forgive the perpetrators. One such story that largely escaped the notice of the press is that of the Travers family. Mr. Tom Travers, a resident magistrate, was attacked by an unknown gunman as he and his family left church after mass. The only apparent motive was that a Republican terrorist wanted to make an example to the Catholic community of "one of their own" who worked in the criminal justice system. Mr. Travers was shot but not killed. However, his daughter Mary, who was walking next to him, was shot dead. A little while after this tragedy, Mary's mother found the courage and the grace to write Cecil Kerr:

> Mary was a young woman full of compassion, forgiveness and love and we know that she forgives, and would want us to forgive, those who planned and carried out her murder and the attempted murder of her dad. We, in the name of the Saviour, would like you to remember Mary and our family in your prayers, and also those who were responsible for her death. We would also like you to pray that all men who have murder in their hearts will be overcome by the love of God so that they, like Mary, will one day be at peace with him. (*WP*, p. 177)

Harry McCann was also a person unknown to history until his tragic circumstances, and grace, thrust him into the spotlight. One morning Harry got in his car to go to work. When he turned on the ignition, a bomb went off, and he became the victim of another indiscriminate act of violence. He was rushed to the hospital, where he recalls hearing a doctor saying, "He's a bloody mess; he'll never be any use for anything." Well, Harry's legs may be gone — amputated at the thighs — but he is mightily useful. I was present at the Christian Renewal Centre when Harry spoke at a meeting. Though it was clearly difficult for him to use his artificial legs, he walked unaided and resolutely, using walking sticks. His cheerful spirit put all observers at ease. His story is quite dramatic, but Harry modestly underplayed the drama. In fact, the force of the blast that hurt him threw him up into the air, and he has had many difficult years following the major surgery he underwent. Harry dismissed all that when he spoke, saying, "Ah, it wasn't easy, but no need to tell blood-curdling stories." He told of the way in which he — not previously a committed Christian — found the grace to say, on the way to the hospital, "Father, forgive them." During his long hospital stay, his inherited Roman Catholic faith took on a new reality for him as he read the Bible and a Catholic prayer book. Today he travels frequently to all kinds of gatherings about forgiveness and reconciliation. After the tragic Enniskillen bombing on Remembrance Day of 1987, a team from the Renewal Centre joined others in comforting the bereaved. One of the members of Cecil Kerr's team was, of course, Harry McCann. Many people think of him as an "icon of grace."

One final testimony from ordinary people will conclude this answer to the question of whether forgiveness and reconciliation are truly possible in this context. At the CRC, on a day of renewal (a day when people from the community are welcome to share in song and testimony), I heard the testimonies of Bridie and Michael McGoldrick. This middle-aged Catholic couple was on vacation (ironically, at Warrenpoint, about two miles from Rostrevor) on July 8, 1996, when their lives changed forever.

When they turned on the TV news, they heard the report that a part-time taxi driver from Lurgan had been killed in Belfast in a sectarian shooting. This young man, also named Michael, was the only child of Bridie and Michael McGoldrick. He had just graduated from Queen's University and was making a little money over the summer as a taxi driver before beginning work. The senseless nature of this random killing of their only child shocked the McGoldricks to the core. All manner of terrible thoughts came to them in the aftermath. At the same time, their hometown of Portadown was the focal point of international media attention, since the marches at Drumcree were imminent. Yet somehow they found the grace to come through this dark time. The McGoldricks believe they received special grace from God, because they freely acknowledge they could not have made it on their own. In the months thereafter, the McGoldricks have found it in their hearts to forgive young Michael's murderers. They admit that their willingness to participate in reconciling work with Protestants at the Christian Renewal Centre has caused some in their Catholic community in Portadown to ostracize them. These ordinary folks are, however, sustained by and sometimes amazed at how their own deep tragedy has allowed them to become channels of God's peace. They are very active in United Christian Aid, a charity that, among other things, ministers to people who have lost children in tragic circumstances. They have gone to Chernobyl and Romania to help others and have pledged to continue to work for peace. When I was in the McGoldricks' presence, listening to their story, it seemed to me that there was less terrible darkness, and more light.

During one of my many visits to the Centre, as I engaged the scene and watched the joyful people, either in praise or in personal conversation, I wondered how they carried on so well in the face of continuing tragedies and atrocities. I asked Cecil Kerr to focus with me on this specific question. Of course he told me of God's sustaining grace that he and Myrtle daily receive. That was the answer I expected to hear. But then Cecil went on to admit that, of course, it was very difficult to come back again and again with confidence after experiencing repeated blows with the suffering people to whom he ministers. Yet, he pointed out, at the moment when news of yet another tragedy seems too heavy to bear, God seems to raise up a person — often a previously very ordinary one — to become an icon of grace. For example, when the Remembrance Day bombing occurred in Enniskillen in 1987, Cecil Kerr was particularly shaken because it was his hometown that was targeted. He led a team from the Centre to minister in Enniskillen. And, he reports, while he and his comrades ministered, they were also ministered to. This is a large part of what keeps Kerr and the people at the Centre going — that in the darkness they always find transcending evidence of God's grace. At Enniskillen, the icon of grace was Gordon Wilson, whose testimony I have previously noted. He exhibited both bravery and grace; as Ken Newell said, "In Gordon Wilson, Christ came back to Enniskillen."

Cecil Kerr has provided, both personally and institutionally, significant leadership in the movement of Christian reconciliation in Northern Ireland. He remains very grateful for the support he has received from colleagues serving in other areas. One particularly good colleague is Ken Newell, minister since 1975 of the influential Fitzroy Presbyterian Church in Belfast. Kerr recalls an occasion when the Christian Renewal Centre joined with the congregation of Fitzroy Church to hold an all-night prayer vigil. They invited, and later welcomed, representatives from all Christian groups. He vividly remembers that night, when those assembled received much encouragement from God and from each other. Kerr quotes what Ken Newell wrote about that evening:

> We are a people made one by
> The love of Christ our Saviour and Lord.
> We have been changed as people by the grace
>   of our Lord Jesus Christ.
> Gone is the pride that desires to dominate;
> Gone is the anger that wants to undermine.
> By his Holy Spirit we want to listen to each other's
>   hurts and fears
> And build together a community fit for us all to live in
> Furnished with the generosity, justice
> and compassion of Jesus Christ. (*WP*, pp. 168-69)

At the end of his novel *Trinity*, Leon Uris wrote, "In Ireland there is no future, only the past happening over and over."[3] Cecil Kerr and his colleagues of the Christian Renewal Centre can understand such pessimism, but their profound conviction is that Uris is wrong. There is a new future for Ireland — a bright future whose signs are already apparent.

I want to conclude this discussion of the Christian Renewal Centre and the members' work for reconciliation and peace by discussing their understanding of their ministry of prayer. In the autumn of 1997, I sat in the meditation chapel of the Christian Renewal Centre with Harry Smith, a senior assistant to Cecil Kerr. Smith's particular calling is prayer. More specifically, he teaches people about

3. Leon Uris, *Trinity* (London: Corgi Books, 1976), p. 900.

97

the nature and function of prayer. Smith is a British Christian who has been at the CRC for seven years. Before that, he spent thirteen years doing fieldwork in Europe for the Health Care Christian Fellowship (HCCF), formerly the Nurses' Christian Fellowship. With the HCCF, Smith had developed a "model" program to teach people about prayer and how to pray effectively. Smith's program answers a deeply felt need among many Christians who might be mature in their Christian experience but be relatively immature in their life of prayer. Smith models and teaches a way to communicate based on a sound relationship with God. His ministry of prayer at the Centre comprises several elements: publishing a prayer newsletter, holding "prayer schools" three or four weekends a year, and taking a prayer-teaching mission to communities where "renewed" Protestants and Catholics together would like to accomplish in their home areas what Smith does at Rostrevor. Smith organized one such prayer group — of Protestants and Catholics alike — in Carrickfergus one weekend in 1994. The group so enjoyed each other's support and fellowship there that they have stayed together to pray — but also to study British and Irish history.

Of particular interest to the concerns of this book is the "prayer school" that Smith led at the Centre in November 1997 called "The Healing of the Nation." Here the regular "method" was employed — of modeling and teaching people how to pray and what to pray — but the focal point in this instance was the healing of the Irish nation. Smith knew that the weekend he chose, November 14-16, was crucial for two reasons: it was the weekend after Remembrance Day, when people stop to remember those who have given their lives for the nation; and it was the tenth anniversary of the bombing of Enniskillen, which had produced the witness of Gordon Wilson. Later, I asked Smith to tell me how that prayer school went. He reported that the diversity of the registrants, in terms of both locale and denomination, was quickly overcome by their cooperative spirit. They experienced the sheer power of common prayer in the midst of a divided society. They learned how to pray for those in authority by using their names and mentioning their roles. They learned how to pray specifically for justice and righteousness in the nation. They learned how to pray for the peacemakers.

No outside observer can say, of course, if Harry Smith's belief is true — that the prayers of the righteous "availeth much." But we can observe the considerable sense of release and empowerment felt by those praying "in the Spirit." These folks doubtlessly joined many others over the next winter in praying for peace in Northern Ireland. When the breakthrough came on Good Friday, 1998, and The Agreement was signed, people who had learned to pray at the Christian Renewal Centre were surely grateful, but they probably were not surprised. Those who pray with such purpose and intensity are more accustomed than most other Christians to having their prayers answered.

There is one final comment to make about Cecil Kerr and the Christian Renewal Centre. Kerr and the CRC have been a great encouragement to many clergy in both Roman Catholic and Protestant churches. Those clergy people who have caught a new vision of what the gospel can mean for reconciliation often face indifference or even opposition in their church communities. Kerr has received many of these folk at the Centre and has encouraged them not to give up and to remain in their churches. This is a role for which Cecil Kerr is largely unsung, as befits a man who is often the one leading others by the Holy Spirit, the most self-effacing person of the Trinity.[4]

4. Author's conversation with Ken Newell, 8 August 1998.

The Columbanus Community
of Reconciliation

The third residential community I will discuss is the Columbanus Community of Reconciliation, located in the city of
Belfast. It was always to Belfast that this book was intended to return. The two previous narratives focused on the communities in
Ballycastle and Rostrevor. But, as the people at both Corrymeela
and the Renewal Centre would insist, they meant for their work,
though they undertook it away from the city, to have an impact
there. The Columbanus Community sees itself in partnership with
Corrymeela and the CRC, and as its ministry has developed from
its founding in 1983, the other two communities have been extremely supportive.

It is also fitting to end with Columbanus because its foundation was Roman Catholic. Of course, it is fully ecumenical now, as
are the centers at Ballycastle and Rostrevor. But, just as we fully
understand Corrymeela only by understanding Ray Davey and his
style of Presbyterianism, and the Christian Renewal Centre only
by understanding Cecil Kerr and his style of renewed Anglicanism,
so we will fully understand the Columbanus Community only if
we come to know the Reverend Michael Hurley, S.J., and his way
of ecumenical Catholicism. But first, a sense of place.

The impression that many people have of Belfast comes via the media. They may have seen street scenes of violence or of people in substandard housing along the Protestant Shankhill Road or the Catholic Falls Road. While there is no doubt that deprived, dangerous areas exist in Belfast, and that such areas are often the scenes of confrontation and violence, there is much more to Belfast than that. Indeed, at first glance, the physical setting of the Columbanus Community almost seems like Corrymeela and the Renewal Centre — a place away from the violence. That impression would be partly true. The large, rambling house at 683 Antrim Road is very welcoming and peaceful. It is set off from a fairly busy road, and with the ample garden in the back, it gives the visitor a sense of sanctuary that is very agreeable. In fact, however, the Columbanus Community has not been far from some disturbing incidents that have occurred further down the road toward the city center. The larger-than-average homes and generous landscaping in Belfast give the impression of a "normal" British city. But the founders of the Columbanus Community fully intended for the community to involve itself in the rough-and-tumble of life in a city divided along sectarian lines.

The person who conceived of and founded the Columbanus Community is Michael Hurley, a Jesuit priest who is one of the most prominent Catholics in postwar Ireland to take up the challenge and disgrace of the divisions in the Christian church. For Hurley, ecumenical activity was not merely a subsidiary undertaking of the church; it was activity vital to the integrity and ministry of the church. Working together with other Christians became a special calling for Hurley, precisely because he believed so completely in the evangelical task of the church. And that evangelical task was more than making Christian converts; it was vitally concerned with poverty and injustice in society, and with war and violence throughout the world.

Over the next several pages, we will get to know Michael Hurley as we follow his journey of faith, which led to the establishment of the Columbanus Community. Like his friends and colleagues — Ray Davey of the Corrymeela Community and Cecil Kerr of the Christian Renewal Centre — Hurley would prefer that we turn our gaze away from him to others: community members Clare O'Mahoney, Margaret Wilkinson, Roisin Hannaway, Paul Symonds, Marion Curtis, Anne Ord, Jannie Nijwening, Nicholas Hammersley, Columba Breen, and the indispensable patrons Gemma Loughra and Cahal Daly. But all agree that Michael Hurley was the person without whose insight and purpose the community would never have come into existence.

Michael Hurley presented himself for "formation" into the Society of Jesus in September 1940. After training in theology in Ireland and Belgium, Michael spent two decades in Dublin as an academic theologian and ecumenist, the first as a lecturer in theology for ordinands in the Jesuit and Carmelite orders, and the second as founder and director of the Irish School of Ecumenics. During the forty years it took this novice to become an internationally regarded scholar and churchman, Michael Hurley did not eschew hard work or hard questions.

As Hurley's life of teaching and scholarship was taking shape, the international Catholic Church experienced a dramatic renewal in the form of the Second Vatican Council. Like many young priests and Catholic lay people, Hurley felt a new freedom to discover new areas of interest and service. He recognized that in his own country the Protestants had taken the lead in matters of interchurch affairs. While continuing to teach conventional theology, he began to develop interests in ecumenical theology and practice; soon those interests would develop into expertise. His public lectures in Ireland, Britain, and North America, as well as his many academic and journalistic writings, made Hurley a scholar and activist of international repute. The 1970s found Hurley first organizing and then directing the Irish School of Ecumenics in Dublin. This was a herculean task. Yet in a single decade, Hurley transformed his idea for an ecumenical, degree-granting center for the study of peace and ecumenism into the reality of an internationally acclaimed institution with a first-class faculty and an impressive list of publications. Hurley resigned from the school in 1980, both because he was sure it could succeed without him and because he knew it must succeed without him. With this background, Hurley looked for a new challenge, one that would lead him, finally, to Belfast.[1]

Hurley had long thought about establishing a religious community adapted to the needs of the day and to the Irish context. Such a community should be dedicated to peace and reconciliation, both nationally and internationally. But it was not until he was on sabbatical after leaving the School of Ecumenics that his mind focused on Northern Ireland. During a long retreat at a religious house in India in 1981, Hurley realized that the community should be located in Belfast. There were many models for his thinking, including communities in Ireland (such as Corrymeela and the Christian Renewal Centre), England, Germany, and India. But the primary model was the Taizé community in France, which Hurley chose because of its international, multilingual witness for peace and reconciliation between Christians.

The winter of 1981-82 was a period of considerable soul-searching for Hurley. His Jesuit superiors had suggested he go to West Africa to head up a new initiative in theological education. But he was fixed on the idea of developing a kind of Irish Taizé, so he asked his superiors for time to explore the feasibility of establishing such a community. He wrote a number of friends for advice and prayer about a community he first wanted to call "Brothers of Unity and Peace" (BUP). As he envisioned it, the BUP community would be based in Northern Ireland, dedicated to work and prayer for unity and peace. The precise kinds of work to be done would be determined ad hoc, on the basis of the members' needs and talents. An ecumenical group of sponsors and trustees would oversee the work. The BUP community would live on contributions and on the earnings of the members. During that winter, Hurley conducted numerous interviews and received letters from many people in Europe and North America. Hurley also had several meetings with interchurch clergy groups in Belfast.

1. Unpublished remarks by Michael Hurley to the Jesuit Community in Milltown, Dublin, 13 October 1990; and conversations between Hurley and the author at the Columbanus Community, 29 January 1991.

With the encouragement of most — but not all — of his correspondents and contacts, Hurley decided to go ahead with his idea. At the strong urging of Dr. Margaret MacCurtain — academic historian and head of the Dominicans in Ireland — he made one major change in his concept: the community would be gender-inclusive as well as denominationally inclusive. So "Brothers of Unity and Peace" yielded to "The Columbanus Community." Columbanus is the name of a younger contemporary of Columba, the famous sixth-century saint of Derry and Iona. The derivative was chosen carefully so that it would be a name that both Catholics and Protestants could acknowledge.

In the spring of 1983 it was decided that Hurley should produce a pamphlet describing the mission of the proposed community and asking people who felt called to such a venture to express their interest. His connection to the Corrymeela Community was important here. John Morrow, then leader at Corrymeela, offered to let Hurley use its Belfast office to interview prospective members. Trevor Williams, leader of Corrymeela since 1994, was then with the BBC. He arranged to broadcast an interview with Hurley, during which Hurley explained both the proposed work of the Columbanus Community and how interested persons might apply. Tom Patterson, a Presbyterian clergyman, oversaw the screening process. It was extremely deliberative, involving both a consulting psychiatrist and a Jesuit retreat director. Hurley did not rush into any aspect of his plan. His Jesuit superiors, noting that diocesan clergy would need to approve of this new community moving on to their "turf," strongly advised Hurley to get the blessing of the hierarchy in Belfast. Just at that time, Cahal Daly was appointed bishop, and, in due course of consultation, the welcome was officially issued. Things moved ahead quickly in the summer of 1983, and seven people — five women and two men (one of them Hurley) — were chosen to become founding members of the Columbanus Community: five Catholics, one Presbyterian, and one Church of Ireland member. A housing search was begun, and when Hurley's efforts at fundraising in Ireland and Germany were successful, the property at 683 Antrim Road was secured. The group of seven founding members moved to Belfast in September 1983, living with friends until the new house could be readied. On September 15, 1983, the first official meeting of the Columbanus Community was held at the Belfast City Mission. It was an ecumenical service of challenge, prayer, and thanksgiving.[2]

The keys to 683 Antrim Road were given to the members of the new community on November 11, 1983, and they moved in that afternoon. These were highly educated men and women: both men were ordained priests, and four of the women had been students at the Irish School of Ecumenics. Of the three communities discussed in this book, this one was founded most intentionally and staffed with the most analytically capable people. They were practical people too, and soon were at work furnishing the old house with used furniture. The three nuns in the Community were very encouraged when a group of young people from the Protestant Shankhill Road came up to Antrim Road and tidied the back garden.

Clare O'Mahoney, a founding member from Limerick in the Republic of Ireland, remembers the first days very well.[3] Not only were the members well-intentioned; they were well aware of what they were doing and of its potential impact. Saint Columbanus, an Irishman from the time of the undivided church, made the following statement in what is now Bangor, county Down, a stronghold of conservative Protestantism: "I cannot understand how a Christian can quarrel with a Christian about the faith. Whatever an orthodox Christian who rightly glorifies the Lord will say, the other will answer Amen, because he also loves and believes alike. Let us therefore all say and think the one thing, so that all sides may be one — all Christians."[4] Clare, Michael, Monica, Eileen, Margaret, Annette, and Malcolm (who came from Australia a few weeks

2. Michael Hurley, "The Columbanus Community of Reconciliation: The Feasibility Study, 1981-83," in *We Plough the Fields and Scatter* (Belfast: The Columbanus Community, 1994), pp. 5-18.

3. Clare O'Mahoney, "Columbanus Community," in *We Plough the Fields and Scatter*, pp. 24-25.

4. Quoted in *We Plough the Fields and Scatter*, p. 24.

later) were hopeful that their collective witness of living together could be a testimony for a church that would once again be undivided.

The first public event of the Columbanus Community of Reconciliation, held on November 23, 1983, was the Feast of Columbanus in the church calendar. It was a joyful celebration. Many neighbors from the immediate area in north Belfast attended the open house and brought food and good cheer. There was television coverage by both the BBC and Ulster TV as well as a radio interview on the RTE, the Irish counterpart of the BBC. The young people from Shankhill Road who had helped with the garden returned with some friends, which added to the gaiety and joyful spirit of the opening day. Also in attendance were representatives of the major Christian faith traditions, headed by Cardinal Thomas O'Fiaich, the Reverend Ken Newell of Fitzroy Presbyterian Church, and David Bleakley, general secretary of the Irish Council of Churches. Still, the celebration was somewhat clouded by recent events. All in attendance were aware that these church leaders, and many others, had just a few days earlier visited the families of those murdered in the IRA attack on a Pentecostal church in Darkley, county Armagh. Perhaps some people in Northern Ireland had grown "accustomed" to IRA and UVF violence, but this incident marked a new low in horrific activity: the assailants burst into the church during its worship hour and sprayed the place with bullets. If those beginning the new experiment at 683 Antrim Road needed a reminder to be realistic — though they were already mature realists — the incident at Darkley served as a stark reminder that the road ahead for the Columbanus Community would be long and difficult. Yet, as Cardinal Thomas O'Fiaich pointed out in his address on that day, Christian hope would win out over despair:

> The inauguration in Belfast today of the Columbanus Community of Reconciliation would be at any time a notable step forward in the path of Irish Ecumenism. But in the present context of violence and polarization in Northern Ireland, it takes on a new and

deeper significance. At a time when some people are saying: "You can no longer trust your Catholic neighbour" (or your Protestant neighbour, as the case may be), this noble and self-sacrificing group of trusting people have such confidence in each other and in the power of God to unite that they are moving in to live with each other. While others are outraged by an inter-Church service even once a year, this prayerful community will come together daily to speak to God in common and to pray for unity in the Church, justice in society and peace on earth. In the very week when a Sunday service [at Darkley] on the Protestant side of the "religious divide" had been sacrilegiously attacked by men who falsely claimed the name of Catholics, God has raised up this living witness to the power of reconciliation, forgiveness and peace.[5]

From the outset, the Community had clearly stated and thoroughly understood goals. It intended to challenge the prevalent sectarianism, injustice, and violence in Northern Ireland society simply by having men and women from different Christian traditions living together in simplicity and peace. The building would provide the facilities, and the members the ethos, in which Christian groups from different traditions might meet — for quiet days of prayer, for example, or for lectures and programs on Christian unity and on peace and justice issues. Among the general goals of the Community, certain emphases would emerge as time went on, both because of specific needs that would arise and because the shifting membership would feel called to respond in a range of ways as they engaged people and society. The developing ministries of the Columbanus Community can best be described by three individuals. I will let them speak in their own words as much as possible to reveal how they understand their callings.

Michael Hurley, the founder and first leader, had a well-established reputation for brilliant academic analysis and for groundbreaking (sometimes controversial) ideas about ecumenism and interchurch activities. As an academic Jesuit, he had little

5. Quoted in *We Plough the Fields and Scatter*, p. 25.

108

prior experience with pastoral duties. As his work at the Columbanus Community developed, he came to see anew the role that forgiveness would — indeed, must — play in political and religious reconciliation in Northern Ireland. On Sunday, October 13, 1985, he gave the following talk, which was broadcast on the BBC:

Here in the chapel of the Columbanus Community of Reconciliation we have a stained glass panel — of a Celtic cross which seems to soar into the skies, with a dove at its foot. It serves to remind us constantly that Jesus, ascended gloriously into heaven, sent the Holy Spirit; that his Church here on earth is the place where his Spirit lives and moves and has his being.

The words "Receive ye the Holy Ghost," St. John 20:22, remind us that this Spirit given to the Church is the Spirit of forgiveness, that a main role of the Spirit in the Church is to forgive. This should not surprise us, because the Spirit is the Spirit of love and peace, and because forgiveness too is all about love and peace. The language of forgiveness does of course suggest otherwise. The etymology and imagery belong to the world of commerce and law. To forgive, to remit, to absolve: these words seem originally to have meant no more than to refrain from exacting a debt or from inflicting a penalty. Now, however, they mean much more. The loving-kindness of the heart of our God, the forgiving activity of the Father, making known their salvation to his prodigal children through forgiveness of all their sins in the life and work of his son Jesus Christ has charged the words with a new meaning. They belong now to the world of love and reconciliation rather than to the world of law and commerce. To forgive is to have no thought of harbouring resentment or of demanding requital, but to persevere in love or to begin to love again. To forgive is, we say, divine. It is an act in which we know we transcend ourselves and the limitations of our mere human nature. Our experience makes it only too clear that to forgive in this new exalted sense could be possible for us only in the power of the Spirit.

The Church is of course a Church of sinners. And we sin not just seven times but up to seventy times seven. It is so easy to forget ourselves and to forget God. We injure and offend God's people, our brothers and sisters. We injure and abuse God's world, our environment and nature. In these ways we offend God himself. But the Church is also the place where forgiveness is preached and practised, where we sinners find God's forgiveness mediated to us in Word and Sacrament, and where we share this forgiveness with others. We are a forgiving people because we are first of all a forgiven people. We can share with others the Spirit of forgiveness precisely because we have first received this Spirit ourselves.

The Church of forgiveness, however, remains a mystery of faith. When recounting the cure of the paralytic and the forgiveness of his sins Mark (2:7) highlights the mystery: "Who," he writes, "can forgive sins but God alone?" Matthew, however, in his treatment of the same incident omits this particular remark and adds at the end: "the crowds . . . praised God who had granted such power to men" (Mt. 9:8). Matthew, it seems, is reflecting the church life of his time, glorifying and praising God for the mysterious fact that a community of mere men and women exists, re-born of water and the Spirit of forgiveness and empowered in that same Spirit to share God's forgiveness with others, indeed with all nations.

When we recite the Creed together, we are proclaiming our belief in the principal mysteries of the Christian religion, one of which is the forgiveness of sins. All of us need to pray that the Lord will deepen our faith in this article of the Church's creed. Happily, events occur quite often which do just that. Indeed one of them coincided with the inauguration of this Columbanus Community, and will therefore always be specially remembered by us. I refer to the marvelous profusion of forgiveness which followed the barbarous Darkley murders in November 1983. But forgiveness is not what Ireland is particularly noted for. In the words of a recent inter-church report, "there is a sense of almost tribal enmity in the Northern Ireland situation, including its politics. This enmity has been inherited from the past and is implacably continued in the present. We seem to have learnt to love only the members of our own community and to hate those who threaten that community's identity." Quite clearly forgiveness is not part of the fabric of our life. In Church and Society we urgently need to create the structures — the rules and regulations, the laws and institutions — which will facilitate forgiveness between groups and between individuals: little things like the wall charts for schools which our predecessors devised nearly a century ago, one of which can still be seen in the old National Schoolhouse in the Ulster Folk Museum; but bigger things too like new political arrangements; all of which, both small and big, will help to melt away the hard lumps within us of resistance to forgiveness. Too many of us have closed the doors of our hearts, our homes, our neighbourhoods, our churches, our organizations for fear of the other side. Today the Spirit of forgiveness, of love and peace, stands at the doors and knocks. If only we will give him entry, he will "take away this murderin' hate" and make of us once again a forgiven and forgiving people.[6]

The gift of hospitality should also be a mark of a Christian community. I can recall taking the bus from the city center up Antrim Road and getting off near the sign for Belfast Castle. I struggled with my suitcase up to the main door of number 683 and was welcomed heartily by Roisin Hannaway, a nun in the Order of the Sisters of St. Louis. It was the first time that I had been welcomed into a home by a nun — although at the time I didn't know her calling because she was wearing "civilian" clothes. During my two-week stay as participant-observer at the Columbanus Community, I was made to feel like a member of an extended family — equally so at prayer, in discussion over meals, and in washing the dishes in the kitchen. Roisin's work outside the Community was with "the traveling people" (those who some insultingly call "gypsies"). Perhaps she finds that the work emphasizes that Columbanus is, for her, a different kind of family. While Roisin Hannaway was not a founding member of the Community, she is

6. "The Spirit of Forgiveness," in *We Plough the Fields and Scatter*, pp. 19-20.

now the longest-serving member, having joined in 1985, and having become the leader upon Michael Hurley's retirement in 1993. She wrote about the vocation of hospitality in an article that appeared in St. Gerard's parish magazine in the autumn of 1991:

In your journeys down the Antrim Road toward the City at the boundary between St. Gerard's Parish and Holy Family you have probably seen our notice "Columbanus Community of Reconciliation. Visitors Welcome!" It's right opposite the sign for Belfast Castle. Older parishioners may remember the house as "Mount Lennox." Bus-users get a bird's eye view of our dining room as the bus pulls up at the stop outside. Having read this article some of you may be tempted to hop off the bus and take the invitation seriously.

So, who are we and what are we about? Although our membership changes as residents come and go we are essentially a small group of people who want to show by our way of life that we openly challenge the divisions in the Church, the inequality and injustice in our society and the violence around us. We want to live by an opposite set of values which we express in our logo as Unity, Justice and Peace. How then do we try to put these values into practice? Well, you need to understand first that we are a mixed Community, in many senses. As members of different Christian denominations, Anglican, Catholic and Protestant, we try to live as an interchurch family, working, eating, praying and relaxing together. As men and women, lay and clerical, of different ages and backgrounds, we work out ways of sharing responsibility, managing funds and making our gifts and talents available to each other and to the wider community. We endeavour to bring all the components of our particular family into harmony, into peaceful co-existence, which is the meaning of the word "reconciliation."

As a family which prays together three times daily, mornings, mid-day and evening, for the realisation of these Christian values we like to think that we provide a good example in the neighbourhood. By simply being together and praying together we hope that we can be like a little candle in the darkness, radiating light and warmth and hope.

Of course, we don't stay at home praying all day. We help other people and organisations in their work towards unity, justice and peace here in the city. So we are involved in a variety of ways depending on the gifts and abilities of our members. For example, Stephanie is out and about encouraging co-operation between our separated schools in Belfast, while Michael runs courses in adult education in conjunction with the University of Ulster. Roisin works with the Travelling people; Paul assists as curate in White-house parish and as chaplain to prisoners in the Maze [the maxi-mum-security prison where many terrorists were held]. Marion cares for the severely handicapped in the Martin Trust, Glen-gormley. Being in the Jewish area of the city we maintain links with the Jewish community and Marion regularly attends the Synagogue.

All of us keep in contact with our denominations and attend our respective Churches on Sundays, for we are not another sect or house church. However, many of us go to a second service on a Sunday in a church of another Christian tradition to learn some-thing of the beauty and dignity of other places and forms of wor-ship. We do have a celebration of the Eucharist, a Mass or a Protestant Communion Service, every weekday. However, in line with Roman Catholic teaching, we yet have to endure the pain of not being able to receive Communion together, a severe depriva-tion for a close-knit family.

You may see posters from time to time in your Church porch or in the local shops advertising events at the Columbanus Com-munity. We run a small centre here, with days of retreat or "Quiet Days," as we call them; we offer lectures and short courses in his-tory, culture and social issues. Last year's Bible Week proved very popular, so we are planning one for next summer, but hope also to hold a number of Bible studies on some Monday nights before and after Christmas.

Having large premises, 683 and 685 Antrim Road, we have quite a lot of guests. There are mostly people interested in learning more about this institution in Northern Ireland and what is being done to alleviate the problems by the Churches and other agencies. Many of these visitors come from England but we do have people of all nationalities, either calling or staying. We have converted the stables attached to No. 683 into a lecture room downstairs and bunk-bed dormitories upstairs for student groups. As you can imagine we often have our hands full and could do with some help from local people.

You may wonder where our finances come from. Well, members pay weekly for their keep and guests generally contribute towards hospitality. We get a grant from the Community Relations Unit at Stormont for running the Centre. Otherwise we depend on donations, on the good-will of many friends and benefactors. Although we do not get financial aid from any Church we do have the support and blessing of the four main Churches. Cardinal Daly and the Church of Ireland Primate, Archbishop Eames, are among our Patrons, as are the past Moderator of the Presbyterian Church, Rev. Godfrey Brown, and past President of the Methodist Church, Rev. Eric Gallagher. We expect to have Cardinal Daly with us on Columbanus Day — 23rd November next, when he will celebrate the Eucharist in our Community Chapel. Our public service of thanksgiving goes the rounds of the local churches each year. This year it will be on the eve of the feast at 7:30 p.m. in St. Peter's Church of Ireland Church, beside the Lansdowne Court Hotel. Bishop Samuel Poyntz will preach at this special Evening Prayer at which you are all welcome. We look forward to seeing many of you there.

Why, indeed, are we named after Columbanus? Well, he is a local Saint of the undivided Church. Those of you whose houses overlook the Lough can see across to where he spent some thirty years of his life at the monastery in Bangor. From there in 590 AD he crossed the sea to France where he set up communities in Luxeuil, and later in Bobbio, Italy. He is remembered throughout Europe as one of the most fearless defenders of Celtic Christianity.

If you wish to learn more about the Community and its activities why not call in sometime and meet "a different kind of family."[7]

Up to this point in our discussion of the Columbanus Community of Reconciliation, we have heard from people in the Catholic Church. And while the founding ethos of the Community is surely a Catholic one, the founders and later members would adjudge their work a failure if it did not make — and maintain — significant contacts with Protestants. Furthermore, among Protestants, the real need was to make contact with Presbyterians, the more conservative and evangelical the better, because it is from that group among Presbyterians (and Church of Ireland members too) that the greatest enmity toward Catholicism and the Nationalist aspirations have come.

Margaret Wilkinson was that providentially provided founding member. She was indeed a Presbyterian, and a conservative evangelical one at that. Her presence during the first decade of the Community's existence lent a quiet credibility to the whole venture. It would not have been newsworthy for a group of Catholics to live together, but for a new community to be able to include a Presbyterian of some accomplishment and acclaim was a noteworthy matter. Moreover, of the seven original members of the Community, Margaret was the only one who was a native of Northern Ireland.[8]

Margaret was born when World War I was at its height. This bright young woman had a good secondary education, and went to Cambridge University in 1936, where she studied English and archeology. Her course in life was determined during her years at Cambridge, and for the next half-century she returned to North-

---

7. "A Different Kind of Family," in *We Plough the Fields and Scatter*, pp. 42-43.

8. These and the following comments about Margaret Wilkinson are drawn from two interviews with her: one by Trevor Barnes, later published in his book *The Wounded City: Hope and Healing in Belfast* (London: Collins, 1987), esp. pp. 104-8; the other by the author at the Columbanus Community on 26 January 1991.

ern Ireland only for vacations and other short stays. As a deeply committed Christian, she was determined to make her life count, both by extending the Kingdom of Christ and by being of service — as her Lord commanded her — to those who could not repay her. During World War II, she worked in England for Inter-Varsity Christian Fellowship, an evangelical student organization, and with the Quakers on the home front. At the end of the war, Margaret went to India, where she served for thirty-six years (until retirement brought her home to Ulster). She worked with the Northern Irish missionary Amy Carmichael at the Dohnavur Fellowship in South India. Dohnavur was an "incarnational" ministry in that the missionaries identified with the people they served. It was a rather radical thing for British/Irish women to do at the height of British dominance — that is, to be part of a religious community of nine hundred run entirely by women who wore Indian dress. Moreover, Amy Carmichael, the founder of Dohnavur, was "ecumenical" before her time. Even though she was a Presbyterian from Ulster, Amy was able to affirm and to work with committed Christians of all denominations. This orientation toward maintaining one's doctrinal beliefs while embracing the need to act gave young Margaret Wilkinson a path to follow in Christian service that allowed her to make common cause with Christians from whom she might otherwise be separated by doctrinal and institutional differences.

Margaret Wilkinson, therefore, gave the Columbanus Community a bit of corrective that perhaps only a person of her background and convictions could give. There is sometimes in the ecumenical movement a glossing over of real differences, either out of a desire to promote unity or out of a willful indifference. Not so for Margaret Wilkinson, who takes her Reformed theology very seriously and will not easily or quickly say that the differences over such things as "conversion" and the sacraments are merely to be ignored. But it has been precisely because she respects her Catholic colleagues so deeply — and asks for the same respect in return — that the living community at 683 Antrim Road has become so compelling. As one Presbyterian elder told me, "It would be all very well to have a bunch of World Council of Churches-type liberals in Community; but it is a matter of compelling interest to have real priests and nuns, committed to their faith, in community with a conservative Evangelical Presbyterian." It is precisely because people like that cannot get along in regular Ulster society that Columbanus has had such an impact.

While Margaret had much to give, she also learned a great deal. She quickly got over the initial difficulty she had with presenting herself as a Presbyterian to mixed audiences, especially to Roman Catholics. What surprised her, though, was the way in which her calling changed at the Columbanus Community. She soon saw that a substantial part of her ministry would be back in Presbyterian and evangelical circles, explaining why it was acceptable for one of their own to be living and working with Catholics. Listen to her explanation:

> When I first came to this community I thought I would spend most of my time at the bottom of the Antrim Road, in a predominantly Catholic area where I could work across the barriers knowing I was united with Catholic people here. But I've come to find that the more worthwhile thing for me is to go back among Protestant people — to missionary gatherings, conventions and rallies — to show them I am still identified with them, that my faith is still basically their faith but that I can live with Catholic people without compromising that faith. That's their great fear. They are afraid that if they appear on religious platforms they will be giving assent to all that the Catholic church teaches. I believe I can recognize a oneness with Catholics in spite of some of the things in their church which I certainly can't accept. . . . There are many small things drawing people together here in Belfast. The candle we light at our prayers here in Columbanus is a reminder of that. But God takes small things and uses them. That's where I see the signs of hope.[9]

9. Quoted in *The Wounded City*, p. 106.

117

Roisin Hannaway saw her calling change in a similar way. She felt her initial calling was to be in dialogue with Protestants. While that continued to be important, especially when she became leader of the Community after Michael Hurley retired and moved back to Dublin in 1993, her most eloquent public statements in Catholic contexts have questioned the exclusiveness of her own tradition.

Roisin is very bright and possesses excellent analytical skills. But she also reveals a passion for the affective meanings of the gospel, and one is not long in conversation with her before knowing how she feels about certain important subjects.

For her, the Eucharist is — as it is for most committed Catholics — the central act of Christian worship because it is the principal means of grace. She still remembers vividly the joy she felt when she received Christ in her first communion. She has been a communicant nearly every day since. The orientation and direction of her life come from acknowledging and receiving Christ in this special way. Such is her religious delight in the sacraments that she was stunned and saddened the first time she attended Mass when non-Catholic Christians were present, and when they had to abstain from what her church could give. It was that experience which propelled Roisin into ecumenical work; that pain of separation at the heightened moment of grace caused her desire for Christian reconciliation to become even stronger. Indeed, she still feels that anguish deeply. Some thirty-five years after Vatican II, her own church has not yielded at all on its claimed monopoly over the Eucharist. So, in the Columbanus Community, the members abide by the division of the churches, and despite their close fellowship, they regularly experience the pain of brokenness at the time they should be one. Listen to Roisin's passionate comment on the subject of the Eucharist and reconciliation:

> We live as a close-knit interchurch family, working, eating and praying together; but at the moment of communion we face the reality of the brokenness of our churches. You find this an absurdity? So do I. The situation angers me, makes me scream out in-

side. I complain to the Lord that it is dreadful, intolerable, unbearable and unchristian, that it is not what God desires. My heart cries out that there must be an end to this alienation because it hurts; it hurts people who want to love one another and to be at one. Reflecting morning after morning I allow my feelings and my intuition to instruct me. There are days when it is my sense of justice which is offended: I look around the Community Chapel aware of the haves and the have-nots, those who are fed and those who are hungry; and I wonder if we are not sometimes celebrating the Eucharist with bread taken from the poor.[10]

Several Catholics have commented privately on Roisin's courage in offering such implicit criticism of her own church, and they find her challenges very persuasive.

Roisin Hannaway told me that her concern for social justice — always keen, as her work with the traveling people attests — has been heightened by her life in an interchurch community. In recent years she felt a growing conviction that it was time for the churches to make public apologies to other communities about how they had all gotten it wrong. Moreover, she believed that it was time for the churches to publicly explore the political meaning of the gospel and how it was wrong to protect terrorists from "our own side" and thus perpetuating violence by keeping silent about it. Consequently, she accepted Ken Newell's invitation in early 1995 to participate in public meetings to be held at Fitzroy Presbyterian Church, in which an interchurch group would meet with Sinn Fein in the morning and with various Unionists in the afternoon. At first, even though she had agreed to go, Roisin felt reluctant. She felt rather "noble," she later told me, about meeting extreme politicians from "the other side" (Protestant), but she trembled at the prospect of meeting those from "her own side." Her person of grace in this respect was Reverend Alec Reid, from

10. Hannaway, "Eucharist and Reconciliation," in *Reconciliation in Religion and Society*, ed. Michael Hurley (Belfast: Institute of Irish Studies, Queen's University, 1994), pp. 189-90.

Clonard Monastery, who is one of the most important behind-the-scenes people in Northern Ireland.

Things got even more difficult for Roisin when the interchurch committee finally got the agreement of a Loyalist political group, the Ulster Democratic Party, to meet. While they would not meet at Clonard Monastery, they agreed to come to 683 Antrim Road. At the time, this was a courageous thing for a Community of Catholic foundation to do, and Roison was delighted to have the complete support of the Community members. There was some uneasiness the night of the meeting, as the presence of extreme Loyalists in the house might have invited a reprisal from extreme Nationalists.

These sorts of discussions between religious and political leaders took place in several locations from 1995 to 1997. Some of the most important breakthroughs came not just when Protestants spoke with Sinn Fein members and Catholics spoke with Unionists, but when religious leaders from both sides spoke to their politicians and encouraged them to do the right thing in the search for peace. While one cannot claim that specific meetings led to the breakthrough on Good Friday, there was a growing momentum in which religious and political leaders participated. When the deadline came, it proved irresistible.[11]

The Columbanus Community has succeeded in ways that even the indefatigable Michael Hurley could only have hoped for in 1983. It has had a powerful impact on ecumenical conversation in Ireland as well as in its local community in north Belfast. It has shown that Catholics and Protestants can live together as a witness for justice and peace.

---

11. Conversation between Roisin Hannaway and the author at the Columbanus Community, 14 September 1998.

Conclusion: A Time to Heal

The beginning of the peace process in Northern Ireland has changed the principal question asked in public discourse. Whereas formerly it was "How can we bring the two sides together?" now it is "Now that the two sides are together, how can they live with each other?" The first was already a challenging issue, but now that a framework for peace has been established, the second proves to be a vastly more difficult undertaking than previously realized. There are so many hurts to be healed, so many wrongs to be righted, and so many memories to be acknowledged that the process sometimes seems overwhelming.

There is no need to revisit our previous discussion about forgiveness other than to underscore its importance now that the peace process is underway. But in the Northern Ireland situation we are talking about more than just contemporary sins and hurts to be forgiven if there is to be reconciliation. We are talking about the memories of two communities with different histories. Every person forms an identity in terms of his or her memories. And persons in groups have a similar and deeply important sense of the past. Indeed, this is what makes personal — and especially social — forgiveness so difficult: the memory of past events. It will do no good to tell a victim to forget about a hurt now that it is long past. It is even more difficult to try to grant forgiveness for those things in the past perpetrated against those no longer living. Which contemporary African Americans will grant a white American's request to be forgiven for slavery? Which living Jew will grant the request for forgiveness for the Holocaust? Which living Catholic in Ireland will accept Britain's apology for the great famine? Which living Protestant in Ireland will grant the request of Catholics to be forgiven for years of terrorist atrocities? The essential problem is that it seems too late to make true amends with those who have been wronged. No act of kindness to a Jew today will bring back the relative of someone — like Elie Wiesel — who smelled the flesh of his people burning in Auschwitz. The victims still alive find it hard to forgive; those already dead cannot. So how can this seemingly impossible kind of reconciliation be accomplished? For forgiveness to actually "work" from the present into the past, we must transcend our own time and place.

Having used the word "transcendence," I acknowledge that God alone can transcend human experience of place and time. In a certain way, forgiveness in politics or in personal affairs implies a religious context in which God — or some transcendent set of values — operates. In this context I find very compelling the work of Gabriel Daly, the Irish priest at Trinity College, Dublin.[1] He has made important contributions to this conversation through his incisive commentary on Iris Murdoch's novel *Bruno's Dream*.

Readers meet Bruno at the end of his long life, in which religion has not played a part. He is thinking back over his unhappy life, and especially his failed marriage to his late wife, Janie. He had been unfaithful to Janie once, and she had reproved him for it for the rest of their lives and resolutely refused to forgive him. Over the years she had called him to her room again and again to berate him. One day when she called him, he sensed — rightly, as it turned out — that it would be the last time. He didn't go because he didn't want to hear Janie reprove him with her dying breath. The decision has haunted him ever since. As the novel

---

1. The following discussion is drawn from Daly's original contribution, "Forgiveness and Community," in *Reconciling Memories*, ed. Alan D. Falconer (Dublin: The Columba Press, 1988), pp. 99-115.

ends, we find Bruno aware of his own imminent death. He still longs for Janie's forgiveness but fears that he will be cursed instead. With the clear-sightedness that impending death can give, Bruno sees that if something deeply matters at the end of his life, it must be the only thing that truly matters about his life. Now he longs for a forgiveness that he fears it is too late to find:

> "If only it could work backwards, but it can't."
>
> Some people believed that too. That life could be redeemed. But it couldn't be, and that was what was so terrible. He had loved only a few people and loved them so badly, so selfishly. He had made a muddle of everything. Was it only in the presence of death that one could see so clearly what love ought to be like? If only the knowledge which he had now, this absolutely nothing-else matters, could somehow go backwards and purify the little selfish loves and straighten out the muddles. But it could not.
>
> Had Janie known this at the end? For the first time Bruno saw it with absolute certainty. Janie must have known. It would be impossible in this presence not to know. She had not wanted to curse him; she had wanted to forgive him. And he had not given her the chance.
>
> "Janie, I am so sorry," murmured Bruno. His tears flowed. But he was glad that he knew, at last.[2]

Gabriel Daly invokes this story to make two observations about the transcendent nature of history — that is, eschatology. First, there is the clarity made uniquely possible by the sense of one's own imminent death. Since Bruno sees clearly the nature of forgiveness, it must be that Janie did too. This suggests that forgiveness has a universal character. Second and more important is the notion that forgiveness must collapse the structure of time and space. If forgiveness is to be universal, it must indeed "work backwards." As Daly writes, "It has to embrace the offence, the offender and the offended. . . . Forgiveness, in short, is both a sym-

2. Iris Murdoch, *Bruno's Dream* (London: Penguin, 1970), pp. 266-67.

bolic mediation of God and a transcendental experience arising out of human limitations. . . . Historically the past is closed, eschatologically it remains open."[3]

This perspective on time and forgiveness is similar to that expressed by C. S. Lewis in his classic book *The Great Divorce*. Despite God's promise to love all and to forgive all because of, and through, the Cross, certain people will choose not to accept God's offer of love and unconditional forgiveness. But, as one looks back on those decisions from the end of time — after the trumpet has sounded — this will cease to be a mystery. For those who have chosen God's real place, so-called "time" will have collapsed, and they will always have been on the way there. For those who have chosen the other place, the same kind of thing will occur: they too will find that they have always been on the way there.

In the context of forgiveness, there are moments of redemption when the structures of time and space collapse, and the reconciliation experienced will always have been so. Such moments are not born of anything so simple as saying "forgive and forget." Rather, the memories of wrong and hurt — when viewed eschatologically, from the end, looking back — will be seen as always on the way to reconciliation, not to violence and hatred. Redemptive moments are possible, and they do happen. Nelson Mandela showed the world such a moment when he invited to his inauguration the man who had been his jailer on Robben Island for twenty-seven years. In this book we have seen the powerful witness of people like Gordon Wilson, Harry McCann, and Bridie McGoldrick, as well as the powerful witness, through leadership, of Ray Davey, Cecil Kerr, and Michael Hurley.

Such moments of redemptive catharsis can sometimes be experienced by a whole community. As I was completing this book in the summer of 1998, the peace process had been well launched. Yet the largest and most devastating single bomb attack in the history of "the troubles" occurred on Saturday afternoon, August 15, in the town of Omagh in county Tyrone. The attack had been per-

3. Daly, "Forgiveness and Community," pp. 102-3.

petrated by a radical faction of the IRA that would not join the majority of its comrades and participate in the peace process. The day following the funerals saw the entire community of Omagh fill the town square in solidarity with the victims and in protest of the madness of violence. This made the men responsible for the attack ashamed enough to apologize and pledge they would not repeat such acts. The tragedy of August 15 will leave Omagh a changed place. I have walked the high street of that charming town several times and even played a round of golf in sight of the parish church. Never did I expect that this hitherto ordinary town would be the scene of such destruction — and of such grace. The people there will always remember their losses, but they will also remember the way they were able to transcend those losses in mutual embrace. Such scenes are glimpses of what the *shalom* of the Kingdom of God will look like when it comes. But when it comes, those who sought it first will know it as having been among them all along.

The time for forgiveness and healing in Northern Ireland has come. I want to conclude with a simple story of the healing of wounds that has profound implications for the healing of Northern Irish people. This story comes out of remarks made at a public hearing held by Sinn Fein in the period between the cease-fires, prior to the Good Friday agreement. Among those who spoke to the Sinn Fein leadership was Dr. William Rutherford, a retired surgeon and a prominent elder in Fitzroy Presbyterian Church, where he worked closely with his pastor, Reverend Ken Newell, on various reconciliation initiatives in Belfast. Dr. Rutherford reminded the assembly that in 1984 the president of Sinn Fein, Gerry Adams, had been wounded by Loyalist gunmen. It was Rutherford who had led the team of surgeons at Royal Victoria Hospital in fighting for, and saving, Gerry Adams' life. The moment was a poignant one, and it was reported in the press the following day.[4] A Protestant doctor had saved Gerry Adams' life. Adams, now healed, could lead Sinn Fein into the political process. Would this

4. "Adams Surgeon Urges Him to Work for Peace," *Belfast Telegraph*, 5 March 1994; "Surgeon Makes Plea for Peace," *Irish Times*, 5 March 1994.

particular event be seen as a model for the healing process for the whole nation? For the Christians of Northern Ireland — Catholic and Protestant — the answer was "yes." The time — and opportunity — for healing, forgiveness, and reconciliation had come.